WOMEN IN JESUS' LIFE

SOORIN BACKER

ABOVE THE SUN

To my husband, Jonathan: Honey-ya, more than anyone else on earth, you have shown me Jesus' love. Our love grows stronger each year. I love you better each day than I did the day before. Thank you for your patience and unconditional love. I love you.

To my Children and my Daughter-In-Love: Austin and Lydia, Kayla, Brandon and Jaden. You are the songs in my heart and the world is blessed to have you. I know you are each destined to change the world for Jesus, and I can't wait to see it happen.

CONTENTS

ENDORSEMENTS

Soorin Backer is a prophetic voice for a time such as this! She receives revelation from the Lord with such profound depth and insight. Her razor-sharp spiritual awareness calls people to a place of emotional and spiritual health while calling forth the destiny on their life. Her desire to see people walking in complete wholeness and defined purpose is what she communicates with her love and actions. She has been a spiritual mama and midwife to me personally and I'm so honored to call her friend and mentor.

The Women in Jesus' Life is a book for NOW. It's time for the women to rise up. Soorin takes you through the personal stories of the women in the life of Jesus. She helps identify the trials, pain, and joy that instills hope to each and every person who reads this book. You will experience Jesus and feel his heart as He calls you into a deeper place of intimacy and realization of His perfect love for you.

~ Julie Nowacki
    Founder and President of Elrod
    Founder and President Convergent Promotions

Soorin Backer entered my life when she asked me to speak at one of her Pearls of Hope conferences. After meeting Soorin and her family, I knew she was herself a pearl – a pearl of wisdom.

In this book, you will discover God's heart for women. Soorin writes well and is able to take you into the history of biblical events in a very insightful manner. In fact, while reading the original manuscript, I was able to learn things I had not heard before.

Soorin shows us the superstitions existing in the context of history and brings to mind the lingering effects of those superstitions that still exist in our day when it comes to our understanding of the true meaning of biblical womanhood.

The women Soorin writes about were used by God to confront injustice in their day and we are invited to do the same in this moment of our history. As you read this book, you will discover forgotten women. They are not forgotten in history, rather, they have been forgotten in reference to God's original intent for their lives. Soorin helps us see that these women did not pursue revenge to rectify injustice and inequity. Instead, they walked forward with honor and pursued righteousness as they established the record of their identity.

I invite you to step into the lives of these unique women through the words of another unique woman, Soorin Backer. You will be challenged, and you will be blessed.

~ Garris Elkins
  Author, Speaker, Mentor

INTRODUCTION

The idea for this book came to me almost a decade ago when I was encouraged to write a devotional for women. This was hard because I'm not an enthusiastic writer, and it takes a lot for me to agree to teach through this medium. When I finally agreed, I envisioned short, blog-style, 90-day devotions of less than a thousand words per day. That seemed do-able. With great reluctance, I sat down to write a little devotional about the first evangelist in the Bible, the woman at the well. I'd always felt so drawn to her. Over the years, my imaginations of Jesus' interaction with her conjured the same scenario and the same questions. The often imagined scenario and speculations streamed out when I finally sat in front of the computer, and I had the bulk of the entire chapter written within a short amount of time. Once the chapter was done, I tried to figure out a way to splice those few pages into a week's worth of devotions.

As I pondered how to make a single character study a series of devotions, I heard a faint whisper in my heart that I quickly recognized as the voice of the Holy Spirit. "Why don't you make this the first chapter of your book and write more character studies?"

Immediately, I said no. Just thinking about writing a book filled me with dread. I said aloud, "I hate writing. Lord, you know there are many others out there who have more to say and can teach through writing so much better than I can."

The Lord graciously suggested, "You could call the book, The Women in Jesus' Life." I remember feeling a thrill with the name of the book. Being a part of Jesus' life is so much grander and better than making Him a part of ours. I googled the title and realized that there was no other book with that title. Softening to the idea, once again, I spoke to the Lord. This time, I bargained with Him. "I'll write ten character studies if you'll give me a chapter a day. I want to be done writing this in ten days. I can't write on the same subject for weeks on end."

Silence. But I felt this peace settle over me. Then, I felt excited. I went to sleep that night thinking of the ten characters who interested me enough to write about. I knew that I wanted to include the five women listed in Jesus' genealogy. The next day, I thought of five more stories that I wanted to explore and five women I wanted to know better.

The Holy Spirit led me to revelations and insights surrounding these women who had often been ignored, and I fell in love with them. What I discovered in my study of the Word, what I felt like the Holy Spirit was revealing to me, rocked my world. I saw that I was never a second class citizen in His eyes. He knew that the world would systemize cultures and religions, even religions bearing His name, to diminish the feminine aspects of creation. And He wanted to reveal that His heart for the "weaker sex" was very tender, very protective, and very empowering. He wanted the world to know that He never creates any person or any class of people to be less than. I wept, I laughed, and my heart soared with joy to know how much God loves His daughters. The Lord was faithful and, within ten days, I had a rough draft.

The first iteration of this book was self-published years ago with little promotion or fanfare. After the first thousand copies were sold, I let it languish and didn't pay much attention to it. In fact, when people asked me about my book, I discouraged them from buying it. I knew that the first version was rough, incomplete, and hastily done. I considered it to be a lost cause of sorts.

However, in recent years, there's been a resurgence of interest about women in the Bible and the role of women in the church. Several friends encouraged me to release this book again to speak into this issue and offer a biblical perspective of God's estimation of women. I had heard from two churches that they'd used this book as a weekly Bible study for women who worked and didn't have the time to do full-length workbooks. As a result, I was invited to speak at a retreat and saw many lives impacted. I still have the sweatshirt from that retreat with the words, "The Women in Jesus' Life" emblazoned on the sleeves.

At the retreat, one woman in her mid-fifties approached me to share that her mother, who was in her eighties, had never read a whole book in her life until she'd been gifted this one. She wanted to thank me because *The Women in Jesus' Life* was the first book her mother had read from cover to cover. She told me that her mother cried when she finished because she felt important to God for the first time in her life. She felt healed of profound cultural and religious wounds in her identity about being created a woman and she was in the middle of reading it for the third time.

The testimonies and encouragement I heard from those who had been impacted caused me to remember why this book was first written and helped me decide that now was the time to release it on a wider scale. In this new iteration, I added more insights into each character, added a chapter on Sarah that wasn't in the original publication, and included thought-provoking questions for individuals or groups to answer. Each chapter also ends with a prayer that includes thanksgiving, repentance, blessings, and declarations.

I believe it's time for both men and women to honor the matriarchs of our faith. Understanding the heart of God for women is absolutely crucial for anyone who wants to be a healthy member of God's family. My prayer is that this book will reveal God's heart so that our hearts will also change. I would like to encourage you, dear reader, to read this book with an open mind and an open heart.

· · ·

Suggestions for Application

As I prepared this book, I aimed for a format that would lend itself to those with limited time. Many people work full time or are young parents raising active children and do not have the energy to read extensively or engage in daily homework. But most of us can squeeze in the time to read 10 pages a week. The chapters are intentionally short and succinct to be ideal for weekly studies individually or as a group.

Each chapter begins with a story. It's a narrative of my imagination based on the biblical passages regarding the characters presented. Each chapter ends with a biblical reference of the story so you can go directly to the source and read the Bible for yourself.

Each chapter also ends with questions about the story you can meditate on. Take some time to reflect and apply the insights presented in the book to yourself and to your personal journey with God. My hope is that this will foster greater intimacy in your relationship with the Lord and bring you to a greater awareness of your God-given identity.

As you read, I encourage you to ask the Holy Spirit what He thinks about the women that He recorded in the Holy Bible. Ask Him why these stories matter. Ask Him what His heart is for women living today. And ask Him how He feels about you and what your role is in healing the fractured Body of Christ.

THE PROMISED

Sarah awakened from her mid-day nap to a loud commotion outside her tent. The day had been unusually hot. They'd sought the shelter of their tent strategically placed in the shade. Even then, the oppressive heat made everyone a bit lethargic. Apparently, while she'd fallen asleep, her husband had been awake, taking in the view of the desert.

She struggled to awaken and shake the slumber out of her mind. She heard Abraham conversing with several men whose voices she didn't recognize. Who in their right mind would be traveling through the desert at this time of day, she thought grumpily. Suddenly, a rush of energy filled the tent, and Abraham was shouting instructions at her.

"Quick," he said, "get three seahs of the finest flour and knead it and bake some bread!"

Before Sarah could answer, he was gone. Out of curiosity, Sarah stood and walked to the tent door. Who were these visitors that they would excite Abraham like this? She saw three men sitting under the shelter of an oak tree and her husband running to the herd of cattle that belonged to them. She was amused to see her elderly husband running in the heat of the day. He would need water after that kind of exercise.

Sarah's gaze turned back to the men under the shade. She made eye contact with one of them. Had he been watching her? An eerie sensation ran down her spine. The penetrating gaze of the man was startling. This was no casual look. Could he read her mind? Her soul felt exposed and naked before him. He saw right through to her innermost being. Sarah quickly broke the gaze and moved out of her tent to awaken the servants. They needed to bake some bread.

As the bread was being kneaded to place before a fire to rise, Abraham came over. He led a young, fattened calf to his servants and instructed them to slaughter the animal.

"Make sure to reserve the choicest cut of meat. I will prepare it myself. Also, send a servant to milk one of the cows. And where do you keep our best cheese?"

In bemusement, Sarah told him where they kept the food and the ingredients needed for cooking.

"Abraham, why are you so excited? Who are these men?"

Abraham stopped and turned to her with an incredulous look on his face. "Woman, do you not recognize the Angel of the Lord?"

A sharp sensation of fear stabbed her heart. "The Lord? What do you mean the Lord?"

"The Lord our God. He has come to visit us."

Sarah's heart beat fast and sweat broke out over her body. "How do you know that is the Lord?" But she didn't really listen as Abraham answered her. She remembered the penetrating gaze of the man who made her feel so exposed and vulnerable. It was undeniable. Her husband spoke the truth.

The next couple of hours moved like a blur as they worked to prepare the best meal possible in the short time they had. The meat was perfectly roasted. There was carefully churned butter and freshly grated cheese to compliment the bread that had just come out of the oven, and fresh milk was poured into their best goblets. They prepared a beautiful tray accented with herbs and vegetables.

By now, the sun was starting to set and the day was cooling. Sarah took her bowl of food and entered her tent, leaving the door open. She could clearly hear her husband conversing with the men. She was glad that they were so near. Curiosity was overwhelming her.

"Where is your wife Sarah?" one of the men questioned.

Sarah's heart leapt into her mouth. They knew her name. Had Abraham told them?

"There, in the tent," answered her husband.

Then, one of them said, "I will surely return to you around this time next year, and Sarah your wife will have a son."

The words struck her deeply, causing her stomach to turn. Were they actually saying that the promise of a son would be fulfilled now? Hilarity hit her.

She thought, *After I am worn out and my lord is old, will I now have this pleasure?*

The ludicrous hope she'd held onto for years had been killed and buried ages ago. She was well past child bearing years and couldn't remember the last time she'd had her cycle. And these strange men were saying she would give birth now? Nay, a year from now. She'd be at least ninety by then. Surely these were false prophets. She clapped her hands over her mouth to stifle the bitter laugh that threatened to escape.

Then, the Lord said to Abraham, "Why did Sarah laugh and say, 'Will I really have a child, now that I am old?' Is anything too hard for the Lord? I will return to you at the appointed time next year, and Sarah will have a son."

Shock went through Sarah. Then, fear struck her. This man had read her mind! He couldn't even see her and he knew what she was thinking and what she was doing. Desperate to appease this supernatural being, she said loudly so that they could hear her, "I did not laugh!"

He answered, "Yes, you did laugh."

Sarah went silent. Her physical senses shut down and the internal turmoil of resurrecting hope, fear of the living God, and the wild yearning for a child of her own swirled. Could it be? If this man could read her mind and see her through the tent walls, could it be that He was truly God and He was telling her the truth? Would she really become a mother at the age of ninety? Could something so crazy, extraordinary, miraculous, and special happen for someone like her?

After all these years, was God finally remembering her?

A Woman's Solution

Most people focus on Abraham. He was the recipient of an eternal covenant that continues to live on today. It's been at least four thousand years since God called Abraham out of a crowd and chose to reestablish a relationship with humanity. Through His relationship with this man, God would show the world who He is and who we are made to be.

Humanity had lost their identity and the purpose for which they were created. At this time, God chose to move through the world and found this one man named Abram. With him the Lord catalyzed His campaign to recover the lost relationship between Creator/Father/God and children made in His image. The apostle Paul tells us in the Book of Romans that the whole Kingdom of God has been grafted into this Abrahamic Covenant.

In all this talk of Abraham and his faith, Sarah is barely mentioned. She becomes an afterthought. Sarah is often portrayed as a weak and mean-spirited woman who rode on the coattails of her husband's faith. After all, Ishmael was Sarah's brainchild, and it was her fault that Abraham didn't wait for his promised son.

When the wait for their promised heir grew too long, Sarai recommended to Abram that they should have her maid, Hagar, carry their child. The whole concept of surrogacy originated in ancient times long before the modern world discovered a way for a woman to be impregnated without sexual intimacy. Of course, many humorous theologians point out that Abram had no objection to this idea. Abram readily complied and slept with Hagar. Ishmael was the result. This happened before God added the Hebrew letter "hei", representing grace, to both their names. It's apparent that it wasn't only Sarai who lacked the faith for the promised child.

8

Abram begged God to bless Ishmael when Sarai remained barren year after year (Genesis 17:18.) But God insisted that the promised son would come through his wife Sarai. After Ishmael was born, the Bible records that Sarai mistreated Hagar and her son. I'm sure when Sarai suggested that Abram have a son through her maidservant, she imagined this solution would bring a measure of joy. She readily opened her marriage bed to another woman to bless her husband and fulfill his yearning for a child of his own.

Sarai would have struggled with the idea of her husband sharing sexual intimacies with another woman as any normal wife would. However, she was willing to make this emotional sacrifice because she'd lost hope that she could bear a child. Rather than deprive Abram of an heir, she sacrificed her own happiness for his sake. I don't think she wanted to mistreat Hagar or Ishmael. Yet, when she had to live out the reality of seeing her husband bond with another woman by sharing a son and watch her husband dote on another woman's child, the personal heartbreak was probably too much to contain.

This is often the case with our own ideas and solutions to divine promises. There are hidden heartaches we can't prepare for and complications beyond our ability to handle. Many of us have promises from God that are yet to be fulfilled. Sarai's attempt to help God along in keeping His promises reminds us that God's promises cannot be forced into fulfillment through our manipulation. The cost is too high.

Sarah's Covenant

Years ago, as I was reading through the story of Abraham in Genesis, it struck me that Abraham did, indeed, have many sons as the children's song says. Abraham had Ishmael with Hagar, Isaac with Sarah, and six more sons with Keturah after the death of his beloved Sarah (Genesis 25:2). He had eight biological sons. Yet, God would call Isaac Abraham's only son.

Preachers like to make the distinction that because Isaac was the only son of promise, he's the only one that counts. Isaac was the only son of a divine covenant. Yet, what I see is that Isaac was actually the only son of Sarah. While Abraham had many sons, Sarah had only one. In fact, Sarah had only one child. It is through Sarah that the nation of Israel would be birthed. God specified to Abram that the promised son must come through his legal wife.

I believe there are two reasons for God's insistence that only a child born from Sarah would be recognized as the child of covenant. The first obvious reason is that Sarah is the actual wife who shares a covenantal relationship with Abraham. God is a God of covenant. He honors relationships that are made in covenant.

God was preparing a generational lineage that would reveal the nature of the Creator that humanity had forgotten. The beginning of this revelation would be that He is a covenantal God. Within covenant, God would reveal mercy and grace beyond our comprehension. His patient endurance and faithfulness towards those with whom He shares a covenant would be illustrated through countless stories of human infidelity and God's merciful response. This journey had to begin with two people in covenant with one another and with Him.

The second reason God insisted that Abraham's promised son had to come through Sarah is a bit more obscure. Women tend to have hidden yet pivotal roles in the Bible. The hiddenness of women makes it easy to assume that women are less important to God than men. In the Bible, for almost every act of faith for which men are commended by God, there is a female counterpart. Though we still refer to Israel as the result of the Abrahamic covenant, upon closer study, it becomes apparent that the Abrahamic covenant is actually a covenant God made with Sarah.

The book of Galatians juxtaposes the covenant of Law and the covenant of Grace. The son of Hagar, Ishmael, is likened to the Law. Ishmael is the result of man's efforts, man's achievement, and man's natural act. Yet, the son of promise was based on God's promise through supernatural means unexplainable by logic. Sarah was years past menopause with no hope to bear a child naturally. Abraham had spent many years trying to fulfill God's promise with Sarah through natural means with no success. Only when God intervened at the right time was Sarah able to conceive a son.

The Alien Versus the Princess

The apostle Paul had the benefit of studying the lives of these heroes of faith. In his teachings, he made it clear to the Galatians that Sarah had to be barren. This couple had to come to the end of human striving in order for grace to be manifest and displayed. They needed to lose complete hope that their natural bodies could create a new life. God was setting them up as an example of what grace looks like.

In the waiting for the manifestation of the promise, a promise that required nothing from the recipients other than to simply receive God's gift, this couple tried to help God. They implemented a solution that would simulate the end result of a divine promise. The Lord allowed the natural outcome to happen. It's only normal for human beings to procreate when two healthy, young bodies of the opposite sex are involved. God endowed men and women with the ability to procreate as an important expression of the divine image we bear. God didn't actively oppose this human solution. He allowed the natural course of events to occur when natural acts were performed.

In fact, the apostle Paul made it clear that it was necessary for the human solution to occur. Human beings are so wired to control the outcomes and to strive for the results they want that God needed to show the world what man's answers to divine promises looked like. God told Hagar that though Ishmael would be blessed, he would live in conflict with his brothers. Not only that, but his descendants would also live in a constant battle against their brothers. Four thousand years later, this prophecy remains true. Over centuries and millenniums, Ishmael's descendants have never learned to live in peace with their brothers.

Human striving without the grace of God always carries seeds of unexpected destruction in the outcome. Ishmael came before God changed Abram's and Sarai's names by adding the Hebrew letter "hei." "Hei" represents the concept of grace in the Hebrew alphabet. Abram became Abraham and Sarai became Sarah. Abram meant "exalted father" and was changed to Abraham, meaning, "father of multitudes, father of nations." The "exalted father" would become the father of many nations after the grace of God promoted him to multiplication.

Sarai meant "she that strives" and was changed to Sarah, meaning, "princess, princess of nations." Sarai propositioned Abram with a natural solution that resulted in Ishmael. After the birth of Ishmael, she quickly realized that her solution had increased her heartache rather than offer solace in the midst of her barrenness. She complained to Abram that Hagar was insubordinate and arrogant. As a result, Abram allowed Sarai to mistreat Hagar and brought greater division and sorrow into their family. All that striving only resulted in greater sorrow for Sarai.

Abram had a son with their Egyptian slave woman named Hagar. The meaning of her name, Hagar, was "the alien, stranger." The apostle Paul takes the analogy of Hagar and Sarah and teaches us the difference between the Law and Grace. Hagar represents the Law. God never intended salvation to come through human efforts. No human striving, solution, or power could bring humanity into the promised land of eternal life. The Law was the product of an alien, a strange source that was never the true Bride.

I've heard the offsprings of the Law referred to as "our brothers from another mother." The Law and the Grace covenant share the same Father. However, the Promised Son that carried redemption for the whole of mankind had to find its origin in death, resurrection, and a divine miracle. The mother who gave birth to the miracle child had to die to self. She could not take credit for the life she would bear and birth. After the death of her natural body which was evidenced in barrenness with no possibility of conceiving, God had to resurrect her body to fruitfulness. God had to also resurrect her heart into a hope that was based on the promises of God. God had to intervene with a miracle and cause life to spring forth from barrenness as a sign that all aspects of redemption have their source in Him. No human ability could be involved other than receiving the gift, carrying the gift, and caring for the gift.

Ishmael and Issac shared the same father. But only one would be a miracle. Only one would be fit to originate the bloodline that would birth the Messiah of the human race. The apostle Paul tells us that only the child of a miracle can carry genuine freedom. Law enslaves because the mother was a slave. She was a slave to natural laws, to human ownership, and to human striving. Grace frees because the mother was free. She was free of natural laws, human ownership, and human striving. One was the result of manipulation that brought greater heartache while the other was the result of divine intervention that brought greater joy. Freedom finds its source in joy.

Unreasonable Blessings

God wanted to show the world what grace looks like. Grace is the essence of unearned, undeserved, unmerited favor. When we study the lives of Abraham and Sarah, nothing truly distinguishes them from the rest of humanity. Abraham is the father of faith, yet this man of faith fell prey to fear more than once. He lied about Sarah to two kings out of fear that they would kill him to take his wife from him. He chose to risk his wife's life and allowed the kings to abduct her for their personal harems.

In one instance, Sarai had to live in the king's household away from her husband for at least a year. We know this because the king realized that his whole household was barren and not a single woman in his entire kingdom was conceiving. That time frame must have been at least a year for them to realize what was happening.

Not only did Abram lie, but Sarai also went along with the lie. She lived in these harems and never resisted what was happening. They both knew that Sarai might have to sleep with these kings. Sleeping with these kings meant risking pregnancy from another man and therefore jeopardizing the existence of their promised son. Yet, neither of them resisted and neither prayed for God to rescue them. It's rather shocking. Especially when we read that Abram had enough men and enough courage to go to war against four kings to rescue Lot, his nephew, when he was captured.

Abram had over 318 men who were trained for war. (Genesis 14) These men were such warriors that they were able to overcome the armies of four kings who had just triumphed over the armies of five kings. This was a huge military victory. Yet, when his own wife was at risk from a single king and his army, Abram didn't fight. He passively handed his wife over to be treated in whatever manner the king pleased. Twice!

Even after God protected him from the Egyptian Pharaoh, Abram would take the same cowardly approach with Abimelech when faced with the same situation. After God rescued them from Pharaoh's harem, Abimelech came for Sarai. He thought her beautiful and wanted her to be his wife. Abram didn't learn from their first skirmish with a king. Sarai didn't learn either. Both of them reverted to deceit and passive acceptance of the outcome rather than remembering that God cared.

Rather than praying and stepping out in faith that God would protect them once again, they submitted to Abimelech's demands. Isn't that just like us? We also have the tendency to forget how God rescued us from so many situations, and we still give in to fear. This couple is so relatable. They don't seem to be extraordinary in their faith.

According to the Bible, Sarai wasn't even angry with Abraham. This plan to lie to the kings that she was Abram's sister in order to avoid war or assassination seemed very logical and right to her. They didn't pray. They didn't trust God to protect them. They didn't fight.

In fact, even when Sarai was in the harem, they never cried out to God for rescue. God had to sovereignly intervene and rescue Sarai and return her to Abram. The first time Sarai was taken, Pharaoh's household was stricken with barrenness. The second time God intervened, He took a much less subtle approach. God appeared to Abimelech in a dream and said, "You are as good as dead because of the woman you have taken; she is a married woman." (Genesis 20:3)

God literally threatened the life of Abimelech, and his entire household experienced terror. Abimelech told God in his dream, "Did he not say to me, 'She is my sister,' and didn't she also say, 'He is my brother'? I have done this with a clear conscience and clean hands."

God answered, "Yes, I know you did this with a clear conscience, and so I have kept you from sinning against me. That is why I did not let you touch her. Now return the man's wife, for he is a prophet, and he will pray for you and you will live. But if you do not return her, you may be sure that you and all who belong to you will die."

Abram was never rebuked or corrected. God only defended him.

Another outrageous part of this story is that God was not ashamed to claim Abram as his prophet even when he was caught in a flat out lie. God defended him. God even informed the king that because Abram would pray for him, his life would be spared. God rescued Sarai. God claimed Abram as his own prophet. Abram and Sarai lied. They put the king's life at risk. They never prayed. Yet, God blessed them. In both incidents, the kings generously gifted Abram with lavish wealth to get him out of their land. They sinned and then walked away with incredible blessings!

The most outrageous part of these stories is not only that God never rebuked either of these people, but He also went so far as to commend them for their faith later in the book of Hebrews. These fearful people, who didn't even pray about the circumstances that tore apart their marriage, are eternally listed in the Hall of Fame of Faith. Pretty scandalous don't you think? I think that's the point.

God isn't looking for perfect people. God is looking for those who are weak and are prone to making mistakes. God is looking for those who are in desperate need of a greater power. He's looking for people who need a good Father. He desires to pour out His grace on weak humanity so that faith is the result of His goodness. Faith is a gift of grace. Faith isn't something we offer first in order for God to act. Faith is a response to the goodness of God that pours out mercy on our sins and lavishes grace on our weaknesses.

What we call the Abrahamic covenant is actually more accurately a Sarahaic covenant. While Abraham had many sons, Sarah had only the one. Abraham offered God other women as options to be the carrier of his seed. God would not compromise. God wasn't interested in other women to be the bearer of the Messianic line. Only Sarah would do. Not Sarah in her prime. Not Sarah in her youth when she had the strength and the energy to keep up with a baby. No, Sarah had to be old. She had to be barren. She had to be years past the age of childbearing.

Sarah had to lose every ounce of hope in herself and find hope in God. God waited. As He waited, Sarah had to wait. She had to watch her husband have a child with another woman. She had to watch as Hagar conceived so easily and so naturally. She had to watch as Abraham took such pride in his son that she could not bond with even when she tried. Sarah had to endure the years of unfulfilled yearning for a child of her own. God was waiting for the end of human efforts. That was the only way those who would read about Abraham and Sarah could understand what grace is.

Those who struggle with infertility understand the pain of striving and falling short. They know what it's like to feel the pain of barrenness when others are busy giving birth, raising children, and growing their families. I had a small taste of what this feels like when it took me almost a full year to conceive my daughter. I had a miscarriage in the midst of that year and I wondered if I would ever conceive again. By the ninth month, I started to feel desperate. Hope was fraying at the edges, and fear was starting to set in. Thank God I did conceive and I am blessed enough to have four children. But I well remember the pain of unfulfilled longing for a baby. I can sympathize with Sarah's heartache.

If there's anything in grace that we can claim as the result of our own effort, performance mentality would quickly devour any sense of gratitude for the divine. Abraham and Sarah had to know that life is a gift of grace. A nation would have to be born from grace. A faith-based tribe of people who know their origin is grace would have to witness to the rest of the world about the nature of God. A Messiah would have to be born of grace to display the inheritance of grace.

Sarah is recorded as a woman of faith because even faith is a gift of grace. God redeemed her mocking laughter that was an outburst of bitterness by naming her son Isaac, which means laughter. God recorded Sarah's life as a life of faith thousands of years later to show us how grace rewrites human history through the perspective of God's nature; not ours. Grace would be displayed at the end of human abilities to show the promise of what God can do in the face of the impossible.

Is anything impossible for the Lord? The answer is no. There is nothing impossible with our God. Sarah got to live out this reality. Sarah's life is recorded and her covenant honored because God is all about grace. She was the blessed recipient of a divine promise.

Going Deeper

1. Do you have unfulfilled promises from the Lord? Just as God was accomplishing something through Sarah during the waiting season, why do you think you're in a waiting season?

2. Have you tried to help God with the fulfillment of His word? Do you have an Ishmael in your life? How did that work out for you?

3. Identify areas of striving in your life that you need to surrender.

4. God rewrote Sarah's history with him and called her a woman of faith in Hebrews. Are there areas in your life you want God to rewrite?

5. Sarah is hidden in plain sight in the Abrahamic covenant. Do you feel hidden? What's God's perspective on your hiddenness?

Prayer of Blessing

Father, thank you for promises of hope in our lives. Thank you that you are faithful and your Word never returns void but accomplishes what it's been sent to do. Thank you for the seasons of waiting, seasons of hope, and seasons of fulfillment. We bless your name and exalt you as the God of covenant. We bring our divine promises before you and ask that you bring about the fulfillment of hidden dreams and desires. As we take great delight in you, we are confident that you bring the desires of our hearts to glorify you and reveal your goodness to the world. We repent of striving and perfor-mance. We want to host your presence and birth the divine promises in our lives. We declare that as your children, we have an inheritance in you. Even our sins, even what the enemy meant for evil, will be used to bless us as we set our sights on you. We declare divine turnarounds, reversals of fortune, and exponential increase of favor and blessings in our lives because we belong to you. Praise the name of Jesus and let all heaven and earth join us as we declare you are the only begotten Son of the Living God.

References:

Genesis 16:1-15
Hagar and Ishmael

1 Now Sarai, Abram's wife had borne him no *children*, and she had an Egyptian maid whose name was Hagar. 2 So Sarai said to Abram, "Now behold, the Lord has prevented me from bearing *children*. Please go in to my maid; perhaps I will obtain children through her." And Abram listened to the voice of Sarai. 3 After Abram had lived ten years in the land of Canaan, Abram's wife Sarai took Hagar the Egyptian, her maid, and gave her to her husband Abram as his wife. 4 He went in to Hagar, and she conceived; and when she saw that she had conceived, her mistress was despised in her sight. 5 And Sarai said to Abram, "May the wrong done me be upon you. I gave my maid into your arms, but when she saw that she had conceived, I was despised in her sight. May the Lord judge between you and me." 6 But Abram said to Sarai, "Behold, your maid is in your power; do to her what is good in your sight." So Sarai treated her harshly, and she fled from her presence.

7 Now the angel of the Lord found her by a spring of water in the wilderness, by the spring on the way to Shur. 8 He said, "Hagar, Sarai's maid, where have you come from and where are you going?" And she said, "I am fleeing from the presence of my mistress Sarai." 9 Then the angel of the Lord said to her, "Return to your mistress, and submit yourself to her authority." 10 Moreover, the angel of the Lord said to her, "I will greatly multiply your descendants so that they will be too many to count." 11 The angel of the Lord said to her further,

12 "Behold, you are with child,

And you will bear a son;

And you shall call his name Ishmael,

Because the Lord has given heed to your affliction.

"He will be a wild donkey of a man,

His hand *will be* against everyone,

And everyone's hand *will be* against him;

And he will live to the east of all his brothers."

13 Then she called the name of the Lord who spoke to her, "You are a God who sees"; for she said, "Have I even remained alive here after seeing Him?" **14** Therefore the well was called Beer-lahai-roi; behold, it is between Kadesh and Bered.

15 So Hagar bore Abram a son; and Abram called the name of his son, whom Hagar bore, Ishmael.

Genesis 25:1-2

1 Now Abraham took another wife, whose name was Keturah. **2** She bore to him Zimran and Jokshan and Medan and Midian and Ishbak and Shuah.

THE REMEMBERED

The day had finally arrived. Tamar had been discovered.

"Burn her! Burn her to death!" Her own family descended on her. Her brothers, her father, yelling, cursing, hitting, dragging her through the tent floor. They called her names and showed no pity. She'd been the cursed one. Now she was the whore, and the whole family would be better off if she was dead. How they'd been so ashamed of her! After so many years of listening to the whole family pronouncing her as a jinx, even her mother, who had initially ignored the curse surrounding her daughter, came to believe that, too. She no longer shielded Tamar from the family that despised her. She wasn't even in the tent to try and stop the men from killing her daughter.

There was no one to protect Tamar. She had to fend for herself. She had to survive. She had to get the men to listen to her and give her a chance.

"No!" Tamar screamed as pain radiated through her body. She wasn't sure which hurt worse, the bludgeoning her body was taking or the burning sting of the rejection from the people who were supposed to love her. She fought the tangle of violent blows surrounding her. Her baby. She had to protect the life inside of her.

That was why she was in this position in the first place. She held her stomach even as she crawled toward the blanket that held the keys to her survival.

She struggled forward, desperate to find her way to the bundle in the corner. Finally, amidst the screams, the bundle was in her hands and she worked to unwrap it. She had to stay curled in a fetal position to protect her baby from the blows directed at her.

"Please, stop! Just look, look at this and take this to my father-in-law. Please, before you do anything more, just show these to Judah. Ask him who these belong to." She panted through tears and sobs.

"I don't care what that is. You have brought more shame to our family, and you deserve death!" The pounding of flesh on flesh filled the tent. She doubled over to protect her stomach while her hands moved to cover her head. The men didn't care. Someone grabbed her hair and started to drag her to the tent opening. "Judah told us to burn you for your sins, and we're here to do just that!"

"Just look!" she pleaded, lifting the bundle with one hand while the other remained as a shield on her head. "At least take a look. Please, just one look!" Tamar continued to beg as her family vented their rage on her with blows and kicks. They had her almost to the tent door, and panic filled her.

"You think this will save you?" her father yelled, his face contorted with vitriolic hatred. "You're a whore, and you will burn!" He finally tore the bundle out of her hands and the cloth unraveled. The contents fell and rolled into plain view.

The seal, the cord, and the staff fell onto the ground. The seal was unmistakable. It belonged to Judah. As recognition dawned, one by one, her family stopped the beating. Silence. The only sound in the room was the sound of her own sobs and labored breathing.

Again, she said, "Please. Just go ask him who these belong to."

Tamar and Her Husbands

What a strange world Tamar lived in. Men could sleep with prostitutes, but when a woman engaged in the same act, she was risking her life. Tamar knew what she risked when she set out to seduce Judah. But she had a purpose that would not be denied. Out of all the women in Jesus' life, I relate to her the least. I wonder how she had the moxie, the sheer guts, to go through with what she did.

Her method for achieving justice is so shady, you wouldn't expect to read the words, "She is more righteous than I," about her from anybody. But that's exactly what Judah said. When he discovered that the baby, or as it turned out, the babies, in her womb were his, he repented.

I used to wonder why she was chosen to be one of Jesus' ancestors. She is the first woman mentioned in Matthew's genealogy. Why does she receive such high honor? When I read her story, I can't help but feel sorry for her. Her first husband, Er, was evil. We don't know what he did. Just that he was wicked and God took his life. Her second husband, Onan, was a conniving user, and he displeased God with his wickedness and he also died.

When Er died because of his wickedness, Judah commanded his second son, Onan, to fulfill his family obligation. The Levirate privilege mandated that if a man died without leaving an heir, the next of kin would impregnate the widow and that child would be treated as the deceased man's heir. This tradition was established to ensure that every man would have a legacy of generational offsprings. To die without leaving an heir was a horrible blight on the family and akin to a curse. Judah participated in this tradition by commissioning his younger son, Onan, to preserve his brother's line and inheritance through Tamar, Er's widow. Onan had no desire and no intention of honoring this tradition. If Tamar bore a son, then, that child would threaten Onan's inheritance because Judah's possessions and land would be divided among the heirs. As was tradition, the oldest son's heir would have received a double portion of the father's inheritance.

Rather than declining to sleep with Tamar, therefore, refusing to fulfill his obligation, Onan pretended to honor the tradition. He took Tamar for himself and slept with her. The Bible records that while he had sex with her, he spilled his semen to prevent any chance of Tamar conceiving a child. He acted selfishly. He dishonored his family and deceived his father. He used Tamar like a prostitute and robbed her of her legal rights. The Lord found this act displeasing enough that the Bible says God took Onan's life. Hence, Tamar found herself widowed once again. Though the Bible is clear that these brothers lost their lives due to their own wickedness, the superstition of the day would have marked Tamar as the common variable that caused the men to die prematurely. She was marked as a bad luck sign, a jinx, or a cursed woman no man wanted to marry. However, Judah still had the legal obligation to honor the Levirate tradition and give her an heir. In a day when women's future and security lay in men's protection, for Tamar to have no child, no son, meant she had no future.

Apparently, Shelah, the last surviving son of Judah, was still too young to father a child. Judah sent Tamar back to her family of origin with the promise that once Shelah came of age, he would send for her so that she could have a chance of conceiving an heir through him. Tamar returned to her family as a grieving widow to not just one, but two men.

Tamar and Her Family

As I read this account and imagine her returning to her father's family, I wonder if her family loved her. Did they show her compassion, or did the superstition of the day prevail and they saw her as some sort of a jinx? I tend to think she was viewed as a jinx. I don't think she received much compassion from her family.

We don't read of any family members protecting her when Judah wanted to burn her for her sin. We read that "she was being brought out" to be burned. They discovered she was pregnant and reported her sin to her father-in-law. Technically, her father didn't have authority over her. She still belonged to Judah's family. She was betrothed to Shelah, the youngest son of Judah, who had a legal obligation to give her an heir.

Rather than protecting Tamar, the family reported her and allowed Judah to decide her fate. Most likely, Judah was relieved to have an excuse to rid himself of Tamar. She had married his older sons and they both died. The common thread, in the superstitious minds of the people of that day, was that the woman they married was the cause of their death. This woman was cursed. What if his last living heir were to die because of this cursed woman? He had delayed in giving Shelah to Tamar out of this very fear.

The Bible tells us that though Shelah was of age, Judah refused to honor his legal obligation to Tamar. When Tamar's family told Judah that she was guilty of prostitution and was pregnant as a result of her sin, he sentenced her to be burned to death. What a terrible, brutal death he assigned her! His hidden rage and resentment against her erupted into punitive hatred.

The family was going to carry out Judah's sentence without any protest. I find that horrifying. Regardless of culture and the prevailing practice of the day, to find yourself being dragged out by your own family with the intention to burn you to death has to be a traumatizing experience. In addition to this trauma, there's the injustice she endured at Judah's hand. She had waited patiently for him to fulfill his obligations to her when she finally realized that Judah had no plans to honor her. She was forgotten. Left alone. In that time and in that culture, this meant no hope of marriage, no hope of children, and therefore, no hope of a future.

Tamar's Desperate Act

When she realized that she'd been jilted, she concocted a scheme to seduce Judah and then sprang a trap. It was not an iron-clad trap since it depended on Judah's participation. If Judah would succumb to temptation and sleep with her, she would have evidence of his sin. If he passed her by and refused to consort with a prostitute, Judah would have shown himself an honorable man. But Tamar would have been left with nothing. She took a risk and gambled. After all, she no longer had any reason to believe Judah was an honorable man.

As the story unfolds, we read that Tamar's bet paid off. Judah did not resist the temptation before him. He saw Tamar by the side of the road and believed her to be a temple prostitute. She must have been exceptionally beautiful for when Judah saw her, he propositioned her and slept with her. It was an impulsive decision because the Bible tells us Judah didn't have any cash on him. Tamar demanded that he hand over his seal, cord and staff so he would have to return to pay her cash. Judah agreed. He had to give her a deposit guaranteeing he would return and make good on his debt.

When Tamar's family came to punish her for committing adultery against Shelah, her betrothed, she strategically provided the evidence of Judah's sin. The family recognized Judah's belongings and was at a loss for their next step. They could not burn her as Judah had commanded. So, they inquired of Judah, "What do we do? Apparently, she is pregnant with your child."

Through a series of events leading from Judah's fall into temptation, Tamar vindicated herself while exposing Judah's disgrace. Though what she did was not honorable, Judah recognized that her intention was. It was for her intention that he proclaimed her righteous. Tamar means "palm tree." Palm trees signified strength, fruitfulness in the desert, and giving of honor. I see Tamar in all of these descriptions.

She had strength and resources. She went after justice and refused to be another forgotten woman. After years of barrenness, loneliness, and the sheer torment of waiting, she finally bore fruit. She conceived twin boys. By doing so, she did indeed honor her husband's family. Though they did not honor her, and all she experienced at their hands was use, abuse, and injustice, she made certain that their lineage was preserved. Through this lineage, the Messiah would come. She chose to be a blessing and not a curse. She chose to pursue righteousness rather than revenge. She chose to be courageous and take a bold risk rather than passively accept her fate. She wanted the child to be from her husband's family. Many like to say she was claiming her Levirate rights to a child, but I think it went beyond the law.

Instead of rolling over and conceding defeat, Tamar fought for her future. She intentionally pursued establishing a future for herself. By doing so, she ensured that Christ would be born through the line of

Judah. She embodied a conquering spirit. In her desire for life, she fought to establish hope for herself.

Judah's Reckoning

Interestingly enough, until this point, Judah had not really distinguished himself from his brothers. In fact, this story is inserted by the Holy Spirit in the middle of Joseph's story. Joseph had just been sold as a slave when we're told this story about Judah and Tamar. Joseph's story is picked up again in the next chapter. What is God's purpose in interrupting the dramatic story of Joseph with this seemingly unrelated story? There are various theories about this. The concept I like the most is the one that camps on the theme of redemption. Judah is redeemed by Tamar's boldness.

We see a man full of bitterness in Judah. He had sold his own brother, run away to a foreign land, started a family with a Canaanite woman. He'd raised sons who freely indulged their wicked nature that resulted in their demise. He eventually lost his wife as well as two of his sons. He also refused to uphold his family honor by ignoring his obligations to Tamar. Lastly, he resorted to indulging himself with a prostitute and had no real sense of honor for his own name.

When he couldn't pay the prostitute, he surrendered his seal, his cord, and his staff as payment for his pleasures without a fight. Essentially, this bundle represented his identity. It's the modern-day equivalent of relinquishing your birth certificate, social security card, and driver's license. These were items that proved his identity. We see a man lost in such depravity he'd completely lost the sense of who he was. Judah's giving up these items that represented his identity was symbolic of a man who had truly lost his way. He'd forgotten he was the descendant of a divinely chosen race, a covenanted people who were to be a blessing to the whole world.

There is nothing about this man, thus far, that would make him the source of the Messianic line. But somehow Tamar's tenacity and boldness broke through his hardened shell. Faced with the evidence of

26

his own sin, he finally broke out in a holy language of humility, saying, "She is more righteous than I."

He came face to face with his own wickedness. He clearly saw his own schemes to rob another of their rights while being outmaneuvered by his victim who refused to be robbed. Tamar acted to ensure that she had her inheritance.

Parents of the Messianic Bloodline

Tamar is not the thief in this story. She is the one who is being robbed coming back to reclaim what is hers. The irony is that what she is claiming as her inheritance is also his. She gave him a gift he did not deserve. In this strange convoluted story of intent, motive, and schemes, we see the redemption of Judah's soul. Tamar offered Judah forgiveness and a chance for redemption when she conceived his sons and restored to him his seal of identity.

Judah would later return to his family. Judah would take the role of leadership among the brothers to make certain Benjamin, the younger son of Jacob's favored wife, would be spared his life. He would shield Benjamin and play the protector. This bond would carry on through the generations for when Israel divided into two kingdoms. Judah and Benjamin remained united. While the lineage of Judah ruled through the bloodline of King David, the Benjamites remained with them in the southern Kingdom. They remained loyal to the Davidic line while the other ten tribes split off and created their own Kingdom in the north.

Judah had sold one brother into slavery out of jealousy and now he was willing to offer himself into slavery to take his brother's place. This was a man who had once gleefully persecuted his own flesh and blood. After Tamar, we see him willing to be the sacrificial substitute so his brother could be set free. It is a foreshadow of the role Jesus Himself would play to save the world. Judah became this man because of Tamar.

Joseph offered Judah the same kind of redemptive forgiveness that Tamar had offered. Though Joseph had the power and the right to punish Judah for his sins, Joseph chose to bless Judah. Not only did Joseph forgive Judah and the other brothers, but Joseph also offered them the best of the land in Egypt during a worldwide famine. Above and beyond mercy, Judah was the recipient of salvation and abundant life. Grace marked Judah's life from the two people he'd wronged the most.

Tamar would never have been mentioned in God's Word if she hadn't pursued justice. She had an overcoming spirit that refused to play the victim. She refused to let misfortune, circumstances, and the wickedness of men define her. She refused to be forgotten by those who were supposed to shelter her and provide for her. I think God liked that about her. I think He likes it when His children fight to capture His attention and refuse to be passed over.

Though Judah conspired to make Tamar the forgotten woman, she fought to be remembered. I think this is precisely why she is included in Jesus' genealogy.

She is being remembered.

Going Deeper

1. Take some time to reflect on Tamar's family. Most likely, none of us come from a family that would burn us alive for our sins. But we might come from a family that lacked genuine love. Do you have traumatic memories from your family that need the healing power of Jesus?

2. List the people in your life, friends or family, you need to forgive even as Tamar and Joseph did. How do you see your life moving forward once you've truly forgiven from the heart?

3. Tamar had a fighting spirit that refused to be overlooked, forgotten, or victimized. What are some areas in your life you need to have this fighting spirit?

Prayer of Blessing

Father, we bless your name. Thank you for inviting us into this relation-

ship with you. Regardless of where we come from, regardless of our family of origin, and regardless of our many mistakes, we know you have a future and a hope for us. We are not defined by our circumstances and misfortunes. We are defined by your love for us. May the comfort of the Holy Spirit heal our past traumas, abuse, and rejection. May all who read this chapter on Tamar receive the blessing of freedom from any bitterness, offense, and hurt. We choose to release forgiveness over everyone who has hurt us and we choose to release blessings over those the enemy wants us to hate. We refuse to partner with hopelessness, bitterness, and depression. We choose to be a blessing to our family, friends, and even our enemies. And out of this place of freedom, we choose to be a blessing that leaves a legacy of life, joy, and peace. Thank you that the death and resurrection of Jesus make this victory a reality in our lives.

References:

Genesis 38:1-30

Judah and Tamar

1 And it came about at that time, that Judah departed from his brothers and visited a certain Adullamite, whose name was Hirah. 2 Judah saw there a daughter of a certain Canaanite whose name was Shua; and he took her and went in to her. 3 So she conceived and bore a son and he named him Er. 4 Then she conceived again and bore a son and named him Onan. 5 She bore still another son and named him Shelah; and it was at Chezib that she bore him. 6 Now Judah took a wife for Er his firstborn, and her name *was* Tamar. 7 But Er, Judah's firstborn, was evil in the sight of the Lord, so the Lord took his life. 8 Then Judah said to Onan, "Go in to your brother's wife, and perform your duty as a brother-in-law to her, and raise up offspring for your brother." 9 Onan knew that the offspring would not be his; so when he went in to his brother's wife, he wasted his seed on the ground in order not to give offspring to his brother. 10 But what he did was displeasing in the sight of the Lord; so He took his life also. 11 Then Judah said to his daughter-in-law Tamar, "Remain a

widow in your father's house until my son Shelah grows up"; for he thought, "*I am afraid* that he too may die like his brothers." So Tamar went and lived in her father's house.

12 Now after a considerable time Shua's daughter, the wife of Judah, died; and when the time of mourning was ended, Judah went up to his sheepshearers at Timnah, he and his friend Hirah the Adullamite. 13 It was told to Tamar, "Behold, your father-in-law is going up to Timnah to shear his sheep." 14 So she removed her widow's garments and covered *herself* with a veil, and wrapped herself, and sat in the gateway of Enaim, which is on the road to Timnah; for she saw that Shelah had grown up, and she had not been given to him as a wife. 15 When Judah saw her, he thought she *was* a harlot, for she had covered her face. 16 So he turned aside to her by the road, and said, "Here now, let me come in to you"; for he did not know that she was his daughter-in-law. And she said, "What will you give me, that you may come in to me?" 17 He said, therefore, "I will send you a young goat from the flock." She said, moreover, "Will you give a pledge until you send *it*?" 18 He said, "What pledge shall I give you?" And she said, "Your seal and your cord, and your staff that is in your hand." So he gave *them* to her and went in to her, and she conceived by him. 19 Then she arose and departed, and removed her veil and put on her widow's garments.

20 When Judah sent the young goat by his friend the Adullamite, to receive the pledge from the woman's hand, he did not find her. 21 He asked the men of her place, saying, "Where is the temple prostitute who was by the road at Enaim?" But they said, "There has been no temple prostitute here." 22 So he returned to Judah, and said, "I did not find her; and furthermore, the men of the place said, 'There has been no temple prostitute here.'" 23 Then Judah said, "Let her keep them, otherwise we will become a laughingstock. After all, I sent this young goat, but you did not find her."

24 Now it was about three months later that Judah was informed, "Your daughter-in-law Tamar has played the harlot, and behold, she is also with child by harlotry." Then Judah said, "Bring her out and let her be burned!" 25 It was while she was being brought out that she

sent to her father-in-law, saying, "I am with child by the man to whom these things belong." And she said, "Please examine and see, whose signet ring and cords and staff are these?" 26 Judah recognized *them*, and said, "She is more righteous than I, inasmuch as I did not give her to my son Shelah." And he did not have relations with her again.

27 It came about at the time she was giving birth, that behold, there were twins in her womb. 28 Moreover, it took place while she was giving birth, one put out a hand, and the midwife took and tied a scarlet *thread* on his hand, saying, "This one came out first." 29 But it came about as he drew back his hand, that behold, his brother came out. Then she said, "What a breach you have made for yourself!" So he was named Perez. 30 Afterward his brother came out who had the scarlet *thread* on his hand; and he was named Zerah.

Genesis 44:14-34

14 When Judah and his brothers came to Joseph's house, he was still there, and they fell to the ground before him. 15 Joseph said to them, "What is this deed that you have done? Do you not know that such a man as I can indeed practice divination?" 16 So Judah said, "What can we say to my lord? What can we speak? And how can we justify ourselves? God has found out the iniquity of your servants; behold, we are my lord's slaves, both we and the one in whose possession the cup has been found." 17 But he said, "Far be it from me to do this. The man in whose possession the cup has been found, he shall be my slave; but as for you, go up in peace to your father."

18 Then Judah approached him, and said, "Oh my lord, may your servant please speak a word in my lord's ears, and do not be angry with your servant; for you are equal to Pharaoh. 19 My lord asked his servants, saying, 'Have you a father or a brother?' 20 We said to my lord, 'We have an old father and a little child of *his* old age. Now his brother is dead, so he alone is left of his mother, and his father loves him.' 21 Then you said to your servants, 'Bring him down to me that I may set my eyes on him.' 22 But we said to my lord, 'The lad cannot leave his father, for if he should leave his father, his father would

die.' **23** You said to your servants, however, 'Unless your youngest brother comes down with you, you will not see my face again.' **24** Thus it came about when we went up to your servant my father, we told him the words of my lord. **25** Our father said, 'Go back, buy us a little food.' **26** But we said, 'We cannot go down. If our youngest brother is with us, then we will go down; for we cannot see the man's face unless our youngest brother is with us.' **27** Your servant my father said to us, 'You know that my wife bore me two sons; **28** and the one went out from me, and I said, "Surely he is torn in pieces," and I have not seen him since. **29** If you take this one also from me, and harm befalls him, you will bring my gray hair down to Sheol in sorrow.' **30** Now, therefore, when I come to your servant my father, and the lad is not with us, since his life is bound up in the lad's life, **31** when he sees that the lad is not *with us*, he will die. Thus your servants will bring the gray hair of your servant our father down to Sheol in sorrow. **32** For your servant became surety for the lad to my father, saying, 'If I do not bring him *back* to you, then let me bear the blame before my father forever.' **33** Now, therefore, please let your servant remain instead of the lad a slave to my lord, and let the lad go up with his brothers. **34** For how shall I go up to my father if the lad is not with me—for fear that I see the evil that would overtake my father?"

Genesis 45:1-2

1 Then Joseph could not control himself before all those who stood by him, and he cried, "Have everyone go out from me." So there was no man with him when Joseph made himself known to his brothers. **2** He wept so loudly that the Egyptians heard *it*, and the household of Pharaoh heard *of it*.

THE REDEEMED

*R*ahab looked out the window and saw the group of men heading her way. The lanterns they carried outlined the spears, swords, and bows in their hands. They were coming down the street at a fast pace. She ducked back in and turned to the men standing behind her. Fear and determination shone on their faces.

"Hurry," she said, "I know the perfect place to hide. Follow me." She darted across the room and climbed the stairs while the men followed her. She led them to the roof where stalks of flax had been laid out in the sun to dry. Removing a bundle, she commanded, "Lie down."

"This offers us no protection. Don't you have a closet you can put us in? They'll be able to see us through this," one man complained.

In an urgent tone, she replied, "You'll have to take your chances here. They're almost at my doorstep now, and we have no time. Besides, they'll check the closets."

The second man had already lain down. Rahab thought this man had more sense.

"Come on, Salmon, lie down already!" the sensible man commanded.

The man named Salmon looked skeptical, but he complied and got down on the floor. Hurriedly, Rahab spread the flax over them as evenly as possible. She shone her lantern over the piles to make sure the men were completely hidden. As soon as she determined they were safe, a fist pounded against her front door. She jumped.

"Open up! We're looking for the Israeli spies, and they've been seen going to your house. Hurry! Open up!" Her body shook with fear.

"Be absolutely still and don't make any noise. They're here," she warned before turning quickly. On the way downstairs, she brushed off the flax from her robe and smoothed her hair into place.

"Yahweh, God of the Israelites, help me," she muttered. She well knew she was risking her life by hiding these men. She opened the door, and the group of men led by a couple of giants barged in before she could say hello.

"Where are they?" the leader growled. He ducked his huge head under the entryway.

"You are housing spies! They were seen entering your place!" The men prowled around her home, searching under her furniture, opening cabinets and closets.

"Yes, the men came to me, but I didn't know where they had come from," she said with a calm she did not feel. "At dusk, when it was time to close the city gate, the men left. They said they needed to leave the city. I don't know which way they went. Go after them quickly! You may overtake them."

"Come on, you heard her. Let's go!" the leader commanded. The mob left in hot pursuit. Relief swept over her and her body shook in the aftermath. Wrapping her arms around her middle, she bent over and let out a huge sigh.

"Thank you," she said aloud. This God must be real. He must be everywhere, for He had heard and answered her prayer. She climbed the stairs to the rooftop. This time, her shaking hands moved a little slower as the terror of the moment passed. She moved the bundles of flax. "They're gone," she said.

The men sat up. Rahab helped them remove the clinging strands of straw. "I know the Lord has given this land to you, and a great fear of you has fallen on us so that all who live in this country are melting in fear because of you."

The men stopped moving and fixed their gaze on her. Looking directly into their eyes, she said with conviction, "We have heard how the Lord dried up the water of the Red Sea for you when you came out of Egypt and what you did to Sihon and Og, the two kings of the Amorites east of the Jordan whom you completely destroyed. When we heard of it, our hearts melted and everyone's courage failed because of you, for the Lord your God is God in heaven above and on the earth below. Now then, please swear to me by the Lord that you will show kindness to me and my family because I have shown kindness to you. Give me a sure sign that you will spare the lives of my father and mother, my brothers and sisters, and those who belong to them and that you will save us from death."

"Our lives for your lives," the one called Salmon answered. "If you don't tell what we are doing, we will treat you kindly and faithfully when the Lord gives us the land."

Rahab searched his face and was satisfied he spoke the truth. She finally said, "Follow me."

She led them to the upper floor of her home, and then searched her house for a rope to let the men down. The men watched in tense silence.

Finally, Rahab found a red rope and tied it to a bedpost. "Go to the hills so the pursuers will not find you," she said, looking over her shoulder at them while her hands worked the rope. "Hide yourselves there three days until they return, and then go your own way."

Again, it was Salmon who answered. He walked over to help her with the rope. "This oath you made us swear will not be binding on us unless when we enter the land, you have tied this scarlet cord in the window through which you let us down, and unless you have brought your father and mother, your brothers and sisters, and all your family into your house."

Their eyes were level with each other, and she sensed strong emotions emanating from him. Fear, tension, and urgency were mingled in his warning. "If anyone goes outside your house into the street, his blood will be on his own head; we will not be responsible. As for anyone who is in the house with you, his blood will be on our head if a hand is laid on him. But if you tell what we are doing"—he grabbed her hand and leaned in, the intensity of his eyes boring into her, as he emphasized his point—"we will be released from the oath you made us swear."

After a moment, his words sank in. She nodded and pulled her hand away. "Agreed, let it be as you say." She stood and opened the window. Her gaze scanned the landscape to make sure it was safe before she stepped aside. She watched the men take turns climbing down the wall of her house using her scarlet rope. After they hit the ground, Salmon looked up and reminded her in a loud whisper, "Tie the rope around the window. Make sure it's visible." She untied the rope from the bedpost and wrapped the cord around the handle on the window, winding it in a knot. "Pull on it, and make sure it's secure," he directed. She made sure the knot was secure by pulling on it several times. When finished, she heard him say, "Good!"

Satisfied, the men ran into the fields under the cloak of darkness. She watched them run until she could no longer see their figures in the night. Rubbing her arms against the chill of the evening, she murmured, "Yahweh, God of the Israelites, remember what I did for your people and show kindness to me." Somehow, she was certain that this God could hear and was taking note of her.

The Unlikely Hero

Rahab puzzles me. She was a prostitute, but she wanted to save her family; brothers and sisters, father, and mother. She was a Canaanite, but she conspired against her own people to help their enemy win. She probably grew up surrounded by gods and goddesses, but she believed in a foreign God that no one had taught her about. She'd only heard stories of the Israelites' God who did wonders no one could have imagined. Bread from heaven, pillar of cloud by day, pillar of fire at night, and enemies defeated by a band of untrained men because they were protected by their God.

I wonder about her. Why did she have to resort to prostitution when she had brothers and sisters, father and mother? Was she a widow and her family refused to care for her so she had to find a way to make a living? Did her family abandon her? Was she sold into prostitution at a young age and had known no other life? Maybe, she was a temple worker in the pagan religion of her day who earned her living by helping others "worship" their gods through sex.

Certain scholars speculate that she was an innkeeper. It makes the reason for the spies being in her home somewhat less suspect. But the word Joshua used to describe her in his book (Joshua 2:17) is the Hebrew word, "zanah" which means "to commit fornication, be a harlot, play the harlot." It's clear that even if Rahab was an innkeeper she also at least "played the harlot."

The natural question that arises is: What were the spies who were supposed to be scoping out the land for the Israelites doing in her home? Would the most obvious reason apply? It's a head-scratcher for sure because the reason for them being in her home is never given.

If circumstantial evidence can be employed, there's no record in the Bible that these men were chastised by Joshua or any of the Israelite leaders for being in her home. Given that this incident occurred years after the Law of Moses was given, it seems highly unlikely that the spies engaged in illicit activities while in Rahab's home. According to Levitical Law, such activities would have been punishable to death by stoning. More than likely, the scholars are right in their theory of her being an innkeeper. And she was also a prostitute. The men may have been staying at her inn while spying on the land, but they did not engage in sin. Perhaps, in order to keep a low profile, they found the seediest neighborhood of Jericho and tried to blend in with the crowd.

As an aside, I find it quite interesting and amusing that Joshua sent only two spies. It makes me wonder if he sent men from his own tribe and Caleb's tribe since the first time they spied on Jericho forty years earlier, only the two of them had given a positive report. He certainly learned from Moses' mistake and stacked the deck, so to speak, to ensure that these spies would bring back the same report that he and Caleb had brought.

Land of Giants

These two men who carried unusual faith, surely would have raised a generation to believe in God's promises. Joshua and Caleb had watched a whole generation of their people die in the desert. A journey that should have taken only days from Egypt to Canaan had taken them forty years! The reason for such a long delay was unbelief. God had to wait for a people lost in a fear-based slave mindset to pass away. A generation of free people who believed in a victory against impossible odds because of God's promises needed to rise up.

Without a doubt, these two elders who were the sole survivors from Israel's first foray into Jericho would have done their best to train the next generation to hold onto faith. I imagine them telling their stories of giants and of grapes the size of their fists. I imagine them pointing to the miraculous wonders they were surrounded by as they traversed the desert. Joshua and Caleb would have done their best to instill and inspire hope and faith. They must have succeeded in teaching the younger generation. The two spies they sent into the land of giants came back with not just a positive report. They came back with a plan. Their faith was absolute. They could take this city because the Lord was with them.

It is an interesting biblical fact that Joshua came from the tribe of Ephraim and Caleb came from the tribe of Judah. These same tribes would later rule the two Kingdoms of Israel when Israel was divided after the death of Solomon. Ephraim would represent the ten tribes in the Northern Kingdom and Judah would represent the two tribes comprising the Southern Kingdom. Joshua and Caleb were honored by the Lord generations later as their descendants became leaders of Israel.

Somehow, the spies' disguises failed them and word spread that these two men were staying at Rahab's place. We don't know how long the two spies stayed in Jericho to scope out their adversaries. But it was long enough for them to be identified by the natives as being Israelite spies. Most likely their foreign speech gave them away. According to Rahab, the whole city of Jericho was on high alert because of the Israelites.

Rahab had a choice. She could cooperate with the authorities and hand the men over, thus proving her loyalty to her own people. Or she could hide these men and ensure that the fate of her own people would include war and defeat. She chose to cooperate with the enemy and keep the spies safe. In return, she demanded a promise from them that when the Israelites invaded her land, she and her family would be guaranteed safety.

The famous wall of Jericho was an impenetrable fortress. Its massive stone wall rose over 3.7 meters high and it was 1.8 meters wide, which roughly translates to 12 feet in height and 6.6 feet in breadth. This wall encircled the entire city of Jericho. No weapon constructed at that time could destroy this massive wall. Jericho itself was populated with warriors, men skilled in warfare, who had established a fierce reputation for themselves. In addition, the descendants of Anakites lived in that land. Anakites were giants known to be over nine feet tall wielding a supernatural strength that normal men could not compete with.

We know that this race of giants survived for hundreds of years after the fall of Jericho because of the story of David and Goliath. David slew Goliath, reported as being nine feet and six inches tall (1 Samuel 17:4), with a sling. Years later, David's Mighty Men slew Goliath's four brothers who were equally gigantic (2 Samuel 21: 18-22). It's really not hard to figure out why the Israelites quaked with fear when they first encountered these giants. It's not difficult to fathom the collective fear the Israelite army experienced when Goliath threw out a challenge for a one on one duel to determine the battle. Not a single man had the courage to volunteer. Not even the king of Israel.

Samuel recorded that Saul was head and shoulders taller than the rest of the Israelite men. As the king and as the biggest champion Israel had to offer, Saul should have been the one to answer Goliath's challenge. Only David, a descendant of Caleb, had the faith of his ancestor. David believed as Caleb had believed. These men had absolute certainty that the God of Israel was mightier than any foe. There was no such thing as impossible odds when God was on their side.

However, these giants were not easy to dismiss. They were, indeed, formidable foes. Practically speaking, Rahab had no reason to believe that the nomadic group of Israelites stood a chance at invading and conquering Jericho. Yet she spoke with absolute assurance that Jericho would fall at the Israelites' hands because she knew that the God of Israel "is God in heaven above and on the earth below." She'd heard of the parting of the Red Sea. She'd heard about the improbable victory Israel experienced against the Amorites. She'd heard stories of miraculous provision and supernatural supply. And Rahab believed.

A Prostitute and Her God

"Faith comes by hearing," Romans 10:17 tells us, and Rahab had heard enough stories to cause faith to arise. Surrounded by idols, demonic worship, myths, and folklore, she could have been like the other Canaanites who trusted in their wall and their gods. She could have dismissed these stories as exaggerated fables and prayed harder to the gods of her land. But hunger stirred in the soul of this prostitute who longed to believe that this God, who had the power to dry up seas, could be the true God of heaven and earth. This was, after all, God's express purpose in choosing to work through the Hebrew nation.

God wanted to manifest His glory to the whole earth through His chosen people so that other nations would know that He is God and worship Him only. But other nations didn't come before YAHWEH and worship. They stubbornly clung to idols and illusions of their own might. In the midst of such hardened hearts, this most unlikely candidate for faith, an uneducated and oppressed prostitute in enemy territory destined to be conquered, a woman who was most likely the marginalized and forgotten among her own people, chose to believe.

Rather than pledging allegiance to her nation and false gods, she chose to pledge her allegiance to the God who was real and to help His chosen people. When she could just as easily have saved herself and forgotten others who had probably abandoned her, she sheltered them under the umbrella of her own faith.

When the Israelites finally captured Jericho, Joshua told the two spies to go and make sure that Rahab was safe. Though some of our English Bible translations say, "Go into the prostitute's house," the original Hebrew word used here is "ishshah" not "zanah." "Ishshah" simply means, "woman, wife or female." Joshua did not define her as a prostitute in this instance. When it came time to fulfill their oath to her, he honored her by simply calling her a "woman."

We see in her a woman who'd probably been searching for the real God her entire life. Idols didn't satisfy, demons didn't snare her, and myths held no appeal. She was waiting for the real God to show up, and when He did, she recognized Him. She chose Him and submitted to Him. She was not righteous because she obeyed the Laws of Moses. She became righteous because, in her heart, she believed God. Rahab believed that Yahweh was big enough, powerful enough, true enough to overcome all He said He would and that He alone would be triumphant.

After the fall of Jericho, Rahab had another choice. Would she strike out in search of a people who had the familiar gods and idols she'd always known or stay with the people who conquered her country and receive their God as her own? Rahab chose to remain with the Israelites and serve their God. By staying and living among the Israelites, she declared her faith to be real. She was not a traitor to her people looking to save her own neck. She truly believed in the God of Israel and wanted to know Him.

Rahab was by no means a woman who a man could bring home to his mother and boast that he would marry. Especially an Israelite mother. But a man named Salmon from the tribe of Judah did. Some Rabbis of old taught that Rehab was so beautiful, that men would climax with ecstasy by simply looking at her. There was something so extraordinary about her, that legends were written of her beauty. I believe this beauty came from her profound faith. The love she had for God so transformed her that even her outward appearance displayed God's glory.

The rest is history, for she becomes the second woman to be named in Jesus' genealogy. With so many Israelite women who were a part of Jesus' ancestry, why is Rahab, a foreign prostitute, so honored? I believe it's because she held out for the real thing. She risked everything to find the One true God who created the heavens and the earth. This wasn't rhetoric for Rahab. Once faith arose in her heart and she knew there was an all-powerful God who could dry up seas, feed the multitudes with heavenly dew, cause water to spout from rock, and quench the thirst of a nation, Rahab surrendered to this God.

She risked her life even as she allied herself with God's people. Her worship and surrender to YAHWEH was real. Rahab was honored, not for her beauty, not for her courage, but for her faith. Because of her faith in the one true God, this foreign prostitute found her redemption.

Going Deeper

1. Rahab had a checkered past that included sexual sin. Do you have anything in your past the enemy is using to keep you from your destiny?

2. Take some time to receive the forgiveness of Jesus over your past.

3. Release forgiveness over yourself.

4. Rahab had to surrender her idols and place her faith in the one true God. Identify the idols in your life that need to be destroyed. (e.g. addiction, bitterness, money, relationships, status, power) What are some steps you can take to make sure you don't return to these false gods?

5. Rahab's faith in God inspired her to hide the Israelite spies. This simple and courageous act resulted in the salvation of her whole family. She also became one of Jesus' ancestors. When you let go of your past and embrace the calling of God in your life, who will be impacted? And how?

Prayer of Blessing

Father, we thank you that you have canceled our sins at the cross. You are the Author and Finisher of our faith and you're the God of second chances. None of us are perfect, and we've all fallen short. We depend on your mercy and grace. We receive your forgiveness as a gift. We haven't earned it, and we are not powerful enough to nullify the power of the cross. We gratefully choose to live our lives in freedom without shame and without guilt. Our identities are not based on our sins; past, present, and future. Our identities are based on the truth that you call us a new creation made in the image of Jesus Christ. We renew our minds daily in this truth and rebuke every lie of the enemy that would steal, destroy, or kill our God-given identity. We are your sons and daughters. We declare our Royalty and bless our families, friends, and our enemies with a legacy of redemption and abundant life.

References:

1.http://www.israel-a-history-of.com/walls-of-jericho.html

Joshua 2:1-24

Rahab and the Spies

1 Then Joshua the son of Nun sent two men as spies secretly from Shittim, saying, "Go, view the land, especially Jericho." So they went and came into the house of a harlot whose name was Rahab, and lodged there. 2 It was told the king of Jericho, saying, "Behold, men from the sons of Israel have come here tonight to search out the land." 3 And the king of Jericho sent *word* to Rahab, saying, "Bring out the men who have come to you, who have entered your house, for they have come to search out all the land." 4 But the woman had taken

the two men and hidden them, and she said, "Yes, the men came to me, but I did not know where they were from. 5 It came about when *it was time* to shut the gate at dark, that the men went out; I do not know where the men went. Pursue them quickly, for you will overtake them." 6 But she had brought them up to the roof and hidden them in the stalks of flax which she had laid in order on the roof. 7 So the men pursued them on the road to the Jordan to the fords; and as soon as those who were pursuing them had gone out, they shut the gate.

8 Now before they lay down, she came up to them on the roof, 9 and said to the men, "I know that the Lord has given you the land, and that the terror of you has fallen on us, and that all the inhabitants of the land have melted away before you. 10 For we have heard how the Lord dried up the water of the Red Sea before you when you came out of Egypt, and what you did to the two kings of the Amorites who were beyond the Jordan, to Sihon and Og, whom you utterly destroyed. 11 When we heard *it*, our hearts melted and no courage remained in any man any longer because of you; for the Lord your God, He is God in heaven above and on earth beneath. 12 Now therefore, please swear to me by the Lord, since I have dealt kindly with you, that you also will deal kindly with my father's household, and give me a pledge of truth, 13 and spare my father and my mother and my brothers and my sisters, with all who belong to them, and deliver our lives from death." 14 So the men said to her, "Our life for yours if you do not tell this business of ours; and it shall come about when the Lord gives us the land that we will deal kindly and faithfully with you."

The Promise to Rahab

15 Then she let them down by a rope through the window, for her house was on the city wall, so that she was living on the wall. 16 She said to them, "Go to the hill country, so that the pursuers will not happen upon you, and hide yourselves there for three days until the pursuers return. Then afterward you may go on your way." 17 The men said to her, "We *shall be* free from this oath to you which you have made us swear, 18 unless, when we come into the land, you tie this cord of scarlet thread in the window through which you let us down,

and gather to yourself into the house your father and your mother and your brothers and all your father's household. 19 It shall come about that anyone who goes out of the doors of your house into the street, his blood *shall be* on his own head, and we *shall be* free; but anyone who is with you in the house, his blood *shall be* on our head if a hand is *laid* on him. 20 But if you tell this business of ours, then we shall be free from the oath which you have made us swear." 21 She said, "According to your words, so be it." So she sent them away, and they departed; and she tied the scarlet cord in the window.

22 They departed and came to the hill country, and remained there for three days until the pursuers returned. Now the pursuers had sought *them* all along the road, but had not found *them*. 23 Then the two men returned and came down from the hill country and crossed over and came to Joshua the son of Nun, and they related to him all that had happened to them. 24 They said to Joshua, "Surely the Lord has given all the land into our hands; moreover, all the inhabitants of the land have melted away before us."

Joshua 6:22-25

22 Joshua said to the two men who had spied out the land, "Go into the harlot's house and bring the woman and all she has out of there, as you have sworn to her." 23 So the young men who were spies went in and brought out Rahab and her father and her mother and her brothers and all she had; they also brought out all her relatives and placed them outside the camp of Israel. 24 They burned the city with fire, and all that was in it. Only the silver and gold, and articles of bronze and iron, they put into the treasury of the house of the Lord. 25 However, Rahab the harlot and her father's household and all she had, Joshua spared; and she has lived in the midst of Israel to this day, for she hid the messengers whom Joshua sent to spy out Jericho.

Matthew 1:5

Salmon was the father of Boaz by Rahab, Boaz was the father of Obed by Ruth, and Obed the father of Jesse.

Hebrews 11:30-31

30 By faith the walls of Jericho fell down after they had been encircled for seven days. 31 By faith Rahab the harlot did not perish along with those who were disobedient, after she had welcomed the spies in peace.

THE BRIDE

*R*uth was so nervous. She didn't know how she was going to go through with this. Hiding behind a tree, she watched the men finish threshing the freshly harvested wheat and head for the table laden with bread and wine. Her eyes focused on one man, the owner of the land they had just harvested. She watched him laughing at a joke his companion had made, and her heart beat a little faster. Boaz looked distinguished, refined, and so handsome. In her eyes, he had that something extra that made him stand out among other men.

Shaking her head, she closed her eyes and groaned. How had this happened? Somehow, somewhere along the way, she had actually fallen in love. Being so emotionally invested made what she was about to do much harder. It would be so much easier if she wasn't in love with him.

The wait was finally over. The men were dispersing and looking for a place to rest for the night. She silently prayed he would find an isolated spot far away from the group. After a few minutes, her prayers were answered. He walked over to the far end of the grain pile and lay down. She waited for a little over an hour until she was certain the men had fallen asleep.

Remembering Naomi's instructions, she tiptoed to where Boaz lay, uncovered his feet, and lay down. Feeling his bare feet against her arm, she was torn between wanting to awaken him and wishing Boaz would sleep through the night. With breathless anticipation, she waited. And she waited. The anticipation slowly wore off. Ruth stayed wide awake while Boaz slept. She felt him move around in his sleep and realized she couldn't bear to leave without knowing. She had to see this plan to the end.

She coughed. Nothing. Boaz was still sleeping. She coughed a little louder. He didn't move. Frustrated, Ruth took a small pebble and threw it by his head. She felt him startle awake. Her heart started to race.

"Who are you?" he asked, sounding alarmed.

"I am your servant, Ruth," she whispered. She sat and turned to face him. She looked down at him lying amongst the piles of straw. The moonlight was bright enough that she could see his startled face.

Sweeping her hair from her eyes, breathless from nerves, she continued, "Spread the corner of your garment over me, since you are a kinsman-redeemer." Did he realize she'd just proposed to him?

Boaz sat up. Ruth saw the tenderness of his expression, and his eyes seemed to glow. Leaning forward, with gentle hands, he swept the remaining strands of hair away from her face.

"The Lord bless you, my daughter. This kindness is greater than that which you showed earlier." He shifted so that, they were sitting hip to hip facing each other. His hand crossed over her legs and landed by her hip, bringing his upper body and his face even closer. Her breath caught in her throat.

"You have not run after the younger men whether rich or poor. Now, my daughter, don't be afraid." He took her hand in his, lifted it to his lips, and kissed the back of it. Her breath left her lungs in a puff. Could he hear the rapid beating of her heart?

He continued to hold her hand, lightly caressing her palm with his fingers. "I will do for you all you ask. My fellow townsmen know that you are a woman of noble character. Although it is true that I am near of kin, there is a kinsman-redeemer nearer than I."

Her eyes widened and her mouth fell open in shock as her heart sank into her stomach. Naomi had not told her this. A small silence passed as they both pondered the full meaning of those words.

"Stay here for the night," he invited, his eyes never wavering from hers. She nodded her assent.

Boldly, she reached out and laid a hand on his dear face. Wild horses couldn't drag her away if this was the only time she would ever be alone with him. Boaz covered her hand with his own. They gazed into each other's eyes. In that moment, Ruth knew that he loved her, too.

Boaz finally spoke. "In the morning if he wants to redeem, good, let him redeem." His voice sounded firm. Ruth pulled her hand away, closing her eyes in shame. She'd been terribly wrong. Rejection pierced her core, making her heart ache. Just when she was ready to rise and run from this shame, she felt his hand on her chin forcing her to face him. He waited until she opened her eyes.

When she did, he leaned in even closer, his eyes looking deeply into hers. "But if he is not willing, as surely as the Lord lives"—he paused, then he continued, emphasizing each word— "I will do it."

Boaz gathered her in his arms and held her as if she was the most precious thing in the world to him. She closed her eyes and breathed in his scent. How she prayed that whoever this other kinsman-redeemer was would refuse her. His shoulders felt so strong and his hands so gentle as he ran them down her hair and the length of her back. Ruth wanted to belong to this man.

"Lie here until morning," he whispered. She nodded again. After a while, he let her go and helped her lie down. Caressing her face, he gazed at her in the moonlight. She had never felt so loved. With a sigh, he moved away and lay down too. But not before he had taken his garment and covered her.

Closing her eyes, she felt tears slide down the sides of her temple, drenching her hair underneath. Her heart ached. "Oh Lord," she prayed inwardly, "let me belong to this man. I've been a bride before, young and ignorant, my husband chosen for me. But now, I have a chance to belong to a man of my choice. A man I already love."

. . .

The Romance Begins

The threshing floor scene between Ruth and Boaz is probably the most romantic story in the whole Bible. For me, there's nothing in the whole Word of God that even compares. There's a timelessness about Ruth's story that sets a romantic's heart ablaze. It has all the ingredients of a terrific love story. You have the beautiful maiden, poor and destitute, working hard to survive. You have a woman of character and nobility who refused to abandon her helpless mother-in-law and selflessly devoted herself to caring for her. She'd been through some heavy trials and suffering. She'd lost her husband, faced famine, moved to a whole new country to live among a people who considered her race to be accursed. She meets the criteria to make the perfect heroine in a romance novel.

Then, you have the hero. Boaz was also of noble character, full of compassion and virtue. He was a man of means with influence and power. He noticed the damsel in distress, fell in love with her at first sight, and swooped in to rescue her. Seriously modern-day romance novels must be based on the Book of Ruth. Believe me, I know something about romance novels. I was addicted to them for years before the Lord told me to stop and I quit cold turkey one day. I had stacks of cheap paperback novels that I donated to the local library.

It's easy to get addicted to romance novels. In a world full of pain, with endings that are uncertain, the formulaic approach of romance novels provides an escape, fantasy, and adventure with a guarantee of a happily ever after. It wouldn't be addictive if the endings weren't guaranteed. The adventure has to be exciting. And, of course, readers want to know it will turn out wonderful in the end. That's the great pay off. There's a longing inside of us that's wired to seek a happy ending. Especially in a woman's heart.

Theologians state that, in the Bible, the Book of Ruth is the clearest typology of Christ and His Bride. That being the case, it's clear to see that our God is a romantic at heart.

Ruth earns the admiration of those who read her story. Her character and loyalty are impeccable. Though she was a Moabite, a race born from incest, she was chosen to be Jesus' ancestor. (Moabites are the product of Lot's daughters having an incestuous relationship with their father in order to secure their family line. The story is found in Genesis 19.) Ruth gives us many reasons to admire her. Her famous words to Naomi, the mizpah, are still legendary. These words of commitment are often quoted by those who know nothing else of the Bible.

"Don't urge me to leave you or to turn back from you. Where you go I will go, and where you stay I will stay. Your people will be my people and your God my God Where you die I will die, and there I will be buried. May the LORD deal with me, be it ever so severely, if even death separates you and me."(Ruth 1:16-17) What a beautiful expression of loyalty and love!

A Woman of Character

This is only the beginning of Ruth's story. She lived out the mizpah without ever wavering. Ruth followed Naomi into a foreign land where Moabites like herself were utterly despised. In fact, Jews had a particular aversion to the Moabites because of their origin. Survival was hard. In a land hit with a severe famine, generosity was in short supply. They were two widows without land, money, and skills. They had no man to offer them protection. Naomi and Ruth were completely vulnerable and dependent on the kindness of others. With no other means of making a living or purchasing food to survive, they relied on the biblical practice reserved for the poor and destitute.

In the days of Moses, God had instructed the Israelites to practice mercy during times of harvest. Rather than taking in the entire field of harvest, Israelites were instructed to leave the edges of the field untouched for those without land to gather food for their families. Many of the poor would jockey for position to glean from these lands. I'm sure Ruth was met with some resistance, name-calling, and racism. In times of desperation when supply was scarce and the needs great, a foreign widow of a despised race would have faced some form of cruelty. Ruth was willing to endure such treatment to support her mother-in-law.

Ruth chose to follow Naomi, knowing what she would face in Israel. She had the option to go back to her family. She would have been surrounded by her countrymen in a familiar culture without the stigma of being a lower caste. It speaks volumes to me of who Naomi must have been for Ruth to follow her to Israel. The Bible tells us that though Orpah, Naomi's second daughter in law, returned to her people, she still wept when saying good-bye to her mother-in-law.

Actually, Naomi had the right to demand that both her daughters-in-law remain with her and take care of her. But this wise and compassionate woman, in her own time of distress, tried to spare her daughters-in-law from further suffering. While Orpah reluctantly left Naomi for the comfort of her own family, Ruth chose to stand by Naomi and serve her. Maybe Ruth didn't have a wonderful family to return to. Maybe she had no better option. Regardless of her situation among her own people, it's obvious Ruth really loved Naomi. Her words of covenant she uttered to Naomi are words born out of love, not obligation.

Naomi was obviously either too old or too infirm to glean. We read that she rested in a cave while Ruth went looking for food. They didn't have enough money to find shelter in a home. A cool cave was their residence while surviving and figuring out their next move.

Ruth was young and strong. She went to the fields as a gleaner and hoped to bring home enough food for them to last one day. Then, she would return the next day to gather enough for that day. Somehow, by divine coincidence, Ruth happened upon a field owned by a man named Boaz.

The Knight in Shining Armor

This man named Boaz was the kinsman-redeemer, otherwise called "ga'el," for Naomi through her husband, Elimelech. Boaz was a wealthy man admired and respected in the land. He probably had his pick of women to marry if he so desired. Yet he'd remained single. It was as if he'd been waiting for the right woman and had refused to settle. He saw Ruth gleaning in his fields, and she immediately caught his attention. He asked, "Whose young woman is that?"

The implication is that he fell in love with her at first sight. Boaz's actions reveal that his heart was fixed on her. He instructed his workers not to harass her and to leave handfuls of grain behind so that she would have plenty to glean. He invited her to his own table and gave her more than she could eat. He was quite older than her. Perhaps, restricted by their age difference, Boaz didn't make any romantic gestures. He found other ways to make his feelings obvious.

Boaz gave her his protection and provided for her. He never pressured Ruth. Once he'd made his feelings obvious, he waited for Ruth to respond. This is a picture of how Jesus relates to us. Jesus doesn't force Himself on His Bride. He waits for her to fall in love with Him. Meanwhile, He provides for her needs and shelters her from attacks. Jesus gives His Bride the power of His name to make sure the one He loves is protected and safe. It's an intense, quiet, unselfish love that doesn't ask for anything in return.

Ruth must have had feelings for Boaz in return. When Naomi instructed her to propose to Boaz by reminding him that he was their kinsman-redeemer, Ruth made no protest. She followed Naomi's instructions to the letter. When Ruth asked Boaz to "Spread the corner of your garment over me, since you are a kinsman-redeemer," she was, in essence, asking him to cover her with his name.

The genealogy of an Israelite man was embroidered on the hem of his robe. The hem of a man's garment represented his identity, his family, and his tribe. For instance, when David cut off Saul's hem in the cave, it was a symbolic gesture that David could have cut off Saul's bloodline if he had chosen to (1 Samuel 24.) Ruth's request that Boaz cover her with his garment was a proposal of marriage. She was asking him to give her the protection of his name.

The role of kinsman-redeemer was quite a risk for Boaz. It would require him to purchase Elimelech's land, (Naomi's deceased husband) with his own money. Then Boaz's firstborn son through Ruth would be considered Mahlon's son. Mahlon was Ruth's deceased husband,

Elimelech's son. The purpose was to continue the name of the deceased and provide an heir. Hence, this son would not be Boaz' heir. Naomi would claim this son as hers. The land that Boaz purchased to redeem for his kin would still belong to Elimelech's family. It's a strange concept for modern-day folks like us to understand.

In Ruth's case, it was a role that the first legitimate kinsman-redeemer was not willing to play. He didn't want to risk complicating his own inheritance and wasn't willing to sacrifice so much for the sake of his kin. However, this was a risk Boaz was quite willing to take for Ruth's sake. He had the right to say no, but he was willing to be her kinsman-redeemer because he was already in love with her. It wasn't the law that motivated Boaz. It was love. There was nothing to be gained by fulfilling the role of the ga'el, kinsman-redeemer. But in Boaz's eyes, the price was not an issue for him. The prize made it worthwhile.

Ruth is immortalized in Jesus' genealogy, in part because she was the recipient of an unselfish love that didn't count the cost. The Holy Spirit shows us through this story that we have nothing to offer but ourselves. Just as Ruth only had herself to offer, so we only have ourselves. Ruth had no money, land, status or societal value. The only thing Ruth had to offer Boaz was her needs. The only way Boaz would have considered her to be of any value was if his heart already belonged to her.

So, it is in God's eyes. The ultimate prize is our hearts. It's unfathomable. The risk doesn't make sense. But true love doesn't count the cost. It focuses on the object of its affections and is willing to pay any price.

Boaz had everything to lose. He was risking his fortune, his land, his name, and his own legacy. It's quite scandalous how much he was willing to risk in order to be with Ruth. There's not even a hint in the Scriptures that Boaz hesitated or second-guessed himself. Naomi said to Ruth, "The man will not rest until the matter is settled today." Naomi proved to be right. Boaz was eager to secure his bride.

Without any delay, upon daybreak, Boaz was at the gate of the city. He called the elders of the city to witness his exchange with the man who was the actual ga'el, the kinsman-redeemer. Boaz offered him the opportunity to buy back Elimelech's land. The man was intrigued. Who wouldn't want more land? Obviously, this man had the resources to purchase the land in question. Then, like a true negotiator, Boaz threw a kink in the alluring proposition.

The man would have to marry Ruth and give her an heir who would inherit the redeemed land. The man lost all interest and surrendered his rights to the land. He didn't want to give away his money, land, or title to another man's family. Even though the son born would be of his own blood, the credit would go to another man. This man surrendered his legal rights in front of witnesses. Thus, Boaz triumphantly secured Ruth for himself.

The story of Ruth really is what every romance novel aspires to. Every woman dreams of having this kind of love. Unconditional. Unending. Unlimited. We want a hero to swoop in to rescue us, to love us with crazy passion and abandon. We want to be pursued, desired, valued beyond measure. Ruth is part of Jesus' ancestry to show us that that is precisely why He came to earth.

He's crazy in love with us. He loves us unconditionally, unendingly, unlimitedly. He is the hero that delivers us from the jaws of the enemy. He cannot imagine His life without us. We are the object of His pursuit, His passion, and the desire of His heart. Jesus redeemed an accursed race born from the heinous sin of incest when He chose to allow Ruth to be in His generational lineage. The Jewish kinsman-redeemer marrying a Gentile bride symbolizes our union with Jesus. In the story of Boaz and Ruth, we see a woman who is considered unclean. Theologically, Ruth was a foreshadowing of the ultimate Bride to be raised up and loved by Jesus Himself. Lost, destitute, rejected, unholy and unclean. The love of one man would exonerate Ruth and make her completely acceptable. In like manner, the Church, once lost, destitute, rejected, unholy and unclean—would find salvation and covenant through the love of Jesus Christ.

Ruth is the ultimate bride. Beloved and treasured. Rescued and purchased. Her hero had to pay a steep price to prove his love for her. That's why Ruth is in Jesus' genealogy. Her story isn't about her noble character. The point of Ruth's story is that she experienced the purest kind of love; the kind that never counts the cost to self. It's the stuff of every bride's dreams.

Going Deeper

1. Ruth experienced tragic loss and profound racism. Have you lost a loved one to death? Have you experienced some form of injustice?

2. Ruth chose to take a risk and go with Naomi when there was no personal benefit to her. Has anyone been this loyal to you? How did it make you feel?

3. Ruth and Boaz exemplified unselfish love. Have you been a Ruth or a Boaz in anyone's life?

4. What season of life are you in? Healing from loss? Laboring to survive? Waiting to be delivered? Living your fullest life?

5. What are some areas in your life that you desire more passion, romance, adventure? Ask the Lord how you can partner with him to invite more life and fulfill His desires for you.

Prayer of Blessing

Father, thank you that you are the deliverer, rescuer, and our ultimate redeemer. Thank you that you own all of creation and you bless us with abundance. Forgive us for partnering with lack. Forgive us for settling for gleaning when you have the whole harvest for us. Forgive us for not preparing ourselves to be your Son's beautiful bride. We receive the blessings Jesus purchased for us. Just as Boaz paid off every debt and gifted land, abundance, and honor, we receive the same from you. We believe you will restore all that we've lost and turn everything around for our good. Ruth went from living in a cave to living in a mansion. We know this is what you have for us. Wherever we have partnered with the enemy's lies that we will always live in loss, lack, and fear, we believe for a divine turn around. We accept that we are chosen to be blessed. We are chosen to be favored. We are chosen to be co-heirs with Jesus Christ. We declare that we have the resources of heaven and it's time to walk in divine favor. We receive your blessings and gifts. We declare we are the bride of Christ, and we are worthy of love.

References:

Ruth 3:1-18

Ruth and Boaz at the Threshing Floor

1 Then Naomi her mother-in-law said to her, "My daughter, shall I not seek security for you, that it may be well with you? **2** Now is not Boaz our kinsman, with whose maids you were? Behold, he winnows barley at the threshing floor tonight. **3** Wash yourself therefore, and anoint yourself and put on your *best* clothes, and go down to the threshing floor; *but* do not make yourself known to the man until he has finished eating and drinking. **4** It shall be when he lies down, that you shall notice the place where he lies, and you shall go and uncover his feet and lie down; then he will tell you what you shall do." **5** She said to her, "All that you say I will do."

6 So she went down to the threshing floor and did according to all that her mother-in-law had commanded her. **7** When Boaz had eaten and drunk and his heart was merry, he went to lie down at the end of the heap of grain; and she came secretly, and uncovered his feet and lay down. **8** It happened in the middle of the night that the man was startled and bent forward; and behold, a woman was lying at his feet. **9** He said, "Who are you?" And she answered, "I am Ruth your maid. So spread your covering over your maid, for you are a close relative." **10** Then he said, "May you be blessed of the Lord, my daughter. You have shown your last kindness to be better than the first by not going after young men, whether poor or rich.**11** Now, my daughter, do not fear. I will do for you whatever you ask, for all my people in the city know that you are a woman of excellence. **12** Now it is true I am a close relative; however, there is a relative closer than I. **13** Remain this night, and when morning comes, if he will redeem you, good; let him redeem you. But if he does not wish to redeem you, then I will redeem you, as the Lord lives. Lie down until morning."

14 So she lay at his feet until morning and rose before one could recognize another; and he said, "Let it not be known that the woman came to the threshing floor." **15** Again he said, "Give me the cloak that is on you and hold it." So she held it, and he measured six *measures* of barley and laid *it* on her. Then she went into the city. **16** When she came to her mother-in-law, she said, "How did it go, my daughter?" And she told her all that the man had done for her. **17** She said, "These six *measures* of barley he gave to me, for he said, 'Do not go to your mother-in-law empty-handed.'" **18** Then she said, "Wait, my daughter, until you know how the matter turns out; for the man will not rest until he has settled it today."

Ruth 4:1-17

Boaz Marries Ruth

Now Boaz went up to the gate and sat down there, and behold, the close relative of whom Boaz spoke was passing by, so he said, "Turn aside, friend, sit down here." And he turned aside and sat down. **2** He took ten men of the elders of the city and said, "Sit down here." So they sat down. **3** Then he said to the closest relative, "Naomi, who has come back from the land of Moab, has to sell the piece of land which belonged to our brother Elimelech. **4** So I thought to inform you, saying, 'Buy *it* before those who are sitting *here*, and before the elders of my people. If you will redeem *it*, redeem *it*; but if not, tell me that I may know; for there is no one but you to redeem *it*, and I am after you.'" And he said, "I will redeem it." **5** Then Boaz said, "On the day you buy the field from the hand of Naomi, you must also acquire Ruth the Moabitess, the widow of the deceased, in order to raise up the name of the deceased on his inheritance." **6** The closest relative said, "I cannot redeem *it* for myself, because I would jeopardize my own inheritance. Redeem *it* for yourself; you *may have* my right of redemption, for I cannot redeem *it*."

7 Now this was *the custom* in former times in Israel concerning the redemption and the exchange *of land* to confirm any matter: a man removed his sandal and gave it to another; and this was the *manner of* attestation in Israel. **8** So the closest relative said to Boaz, "Buy *it* for yourself." And he removed his sandal. **9** Then Boaz said to the elders and all the people, "You are witnesses today that I have bought from the hand of Naomi all that belonged to Elimelech and all that belonged to Chilion and Mahlon. **10** Moreover, I have acquired Ruth the Moabitess, the widow of Mahlon, to be my wife in order to raise up the name of the deceased on his inheritance, so that the name of the deceased will not be cut off from his brothers or from the court of his *birth* place; you are witnesses today." **11** All the people who were in the court, and the elders, said, "*We are* witnesses. May the Lord make the woman who is coming into your home like Rachel and Leah, both of whom built the house of Israel; and may you achieve wealth in Ephrathah and become famous in Bethlehem. **12** Moreover, may your house be like the house of Perez whom Tamar bore to Judah, through the offspring which the Lord will give you by this young woman."

13 So Boaz took Ruth, and she became his wife, and he went in to her. And the Lord enabled her to conceive, and she gave birth to a son. **14** Then the women said to Naomi, "Blessed is the Lord who has not left you without a redeemer today, and may his name become famous in Israel. **15** May he also be to you a restorer of life and a sustainer of your old age; for your daughter-in-law, who loves you and is better to you than seven sons, has given birth to him."

Ruth 4:16-21

The Genealogy of David

16 Then Naomi took the child and laid him in her lap, and became his nurse. **17** The neighbor women gave him a name, saying, "A son has been born to Naomi!" So they named him Obed. He is the father of Jesse, the father of David.

THE QUEEN

*T*he midwife's urgent words of encouragement broke through her wall of pain. "That's it. You're almost done. I see the head!"

Bathsheba fisted her hands around the sheets and prepared to bear down again. Sweat poured into her eyes as another wave of contractions washed over her. The pain was unbearable.

"Aaaahhhh!!!" she cried out, writhing in agony.

"No, don't give up. It's time to push now. Push! You're almost there. There...yes...like that!"

Clenching her teeth, her head tucked into her chest, Bathsheba pushed with all her might. She felt the swoosh of the baby leaving her body.

"Yes! You did it!" the mid-wife announced with joy.

Half sobbing, half laughing, Bathsheba fell back as her spent body went limp. She felt lighter already. The afterbirth would come, but the hardest part was over.

"What is it?" she asked eagerly. "Boy, girl? Is the baby healthy? Why don't I hear the baby crying?" Even as she finished that sentence, she heard the wail of an infant fill the room. Joy exploded inside of her. Her baby!

"It's a boy, dear Queen. You have yourself a healthy baby boy." The midwife and the maid broke out in laughter. The baby's wails grew louder.

"Ah, he's a healthy one, and he wants his mother. Just a minute, precious. We'll get you cleaned up."

Bathsheba prayed inwardly. *Oh please, God, let him live, she begged. Let him live. Do not let this one pay for our sins. If you must take someone, Lord, take me. But let this one live.*

Tears welled and spilled down the sides of her face. She couldn't help remembering her firstborn son. The son who had paid with his life for his parents' sin. How she still grieved for that little one. But he was gone. Now was the time to fight, to pray, to contend for this newborn son.

"Let me see him," she said eagerly as fresh strength filled her. She lifted her head and saw the midwife wrapping the baby in a soft cloth. Her son was still complaining about the discomfort of the world after leaving the warmth of his mother's womb. Finally, they brought the precious bundle to her. She laughed to hear him cry. His little mouth was open so wide in protest that it made a little square. He looked so much like his brother.

"We must tell the king," the midwife said. She directed the maid next to her, "Go tell the king he has another son."

Bathsheba barely heard, as she kept her gaze intently fixed on her son. *Oh Lord, God of heaven and earth, you hold everything in your hands and nothing is impossible for you. Please, God, please let this one live.*

A Mother's Grief

One of life's greatest sorrows that a person can live through is to lose a child to death. Of course, losing any loved one throws us into the tumult of grief, but when a parent loses a child, there's an unnaturalness to the experience that makes it even more horrendous. The order of nature is shifted, and the elder finds themself surviving the young. The survivor's guilt that mourners naturally experience must be especially intense for a parent. But what happens if the baby died because of the parent's wrongdoing? What if the baby's death really was the parent's fault? How does the parent live through in a situation like that?

David and Bathsheba shared the horror of losing their first newborn son. Their first son was born as a result of sin. A prophet came to pronounce judgment that due to his transgression, David would lose his son. For a week, the infant lived. Then the prophet's words came to pass.

We know how David dealt with his grief because the Bible tells us. He wept, fasted, and prayed for seven days while his son was dying. When news of his son's death reached him, David rose from prayer, bathed, and put on lotions. He asked that a meal be brought to him and ate. He had grieved before the baby died.

We don't know what Bathsheba went through. It's harder for fathers to bond with an unborn child. They are not the ones carrying the baby, getting to know their temperament before they're even born. Mothers who have given birth to more than one child can tell you how each baby's personality manifests even during the pregnancy. It's easier to bond and love your baby when he or she is growing inside of you. It makes perfect sense that when an infant dies, it's normal to have the mom experience a level of grief that the dad doesn't. Given that, I think it's safe to assume that Bathsheba's grief over the death of her firstborn son would have been very different from what David experienced.

She held her son for seven days before he died. Imagine being pregnant. A revered prophet had already come to pronounce that her baby would die because of her sin long before she had given birth. How would she have spent that time as her belly grew and she felt the life of her baby growing in her? How would she have dealt with the agony and the joy of childbirth?

Bathsheba held her baby, watched him fade away, knowing he was destined to die. He wasn't dying because of any natural illness, but a judgment had been pronounced. This baby would pay the price for his parents' sin. What did she go through when that baby took his last breath and the finality of death took him away from her? How did she view God?

That last question is difficult to answer. Her story is told in an indirect manner. David is the focus of the story, and we have to infer Bathsheba's journey through her interactions with other characters.

Uriah had been one of David's Mighty Men called "The Thirty." This group of Thirty Mighty Men were icons in their own time. Each became a member of this exclusive group because of the heroics they achieved on the battlefield. Some were credited with slaying hundreds of men on their own during a single battle while others led their troops to victories against all odds. These were no ordinary warriors. They truly were the stuff of legends, myths, and songs. They stood by their leader in exile, living in the land of their enemies, the Philistines. These men hid in caves with David while being pursued by the leader of their nation long before David was accepted as King over Israel. The life and death loyalty of these men toward David was extraordinary.

Absalom's Connection

Bathsheba's grandfather, Ahitophel, was a shrewd military/political counselor. The Bible tells us that Ahitophel's counsel was counted as wisdom from God Himself. He'd been a valued member of David's counsel who unexpectedly defected to Absalom's camp. Not many years after David married Bathsheba, David's own son, Absalom, attempted to overthrow his father's kingdom.

David assigned his friend, Hushai, to act as a double agent for him and spy on Absalom when he realized Ahitophel would be counseling his son. David was forced to abandon his castle and run to the shelter of caves. Before David had been anointed king over Israel, he'd spent years hiding from Saul in the mountains surrounding Jerusalem. Once again, years into his established kingdom, David was fleeing for his life. However, this time, David was running from his own son.

Absalom had grown bitter against his father. His beautiful sister, Tamar, had been raped by their half brother. Amnon, the perpetrator of incest and rape, was David's oldest son and the heir to the throne. Instead of dealing with the issues as a father should, David ignored what Amnon had done. In a time and culture when a woman's honor was tied to her virginity and she was completely vulnerable without a man's protection, Amnon's despicable treatment of Tamar had effectively ruined any chances of a future for her. Tamar grieved loudly in sackcloth and ashes until Absalom came to her rescue.

Absalom was a good brother. He loved his sister and sheltered her when David should have been the one to do so. When Absalom had a daughter, he even named his baby after his bereaved sister. He waited for his father to avenge his sister and hold Amnon accountable for his actions. David did not come through. He continued to ignore the issue, and Amnon continued as the reigning heir to the throne.

Eventually, Absalom conspired to kill Amnon and succeeded in murdering his brother. Rather than answering this heinous crime of murder as a king and a father should, David's response was to ban Absalom from Israel. Mosaic law demanded that Absalom be stoned to death for his crime. Yet, David didn't address the severity of the crime with an appropriate punishment. Once again, he ignored the law of the land and swept the issue aside. David failed as a king and a father. Meanwhile, Absalom's bitterness against his father grew.

After a few years of banishment, Absalom demanded an audience with the king. When David refused, Absalom forced the issue by setting fire to a field. Again, David showed his weakness as a father when he ceded to Absalom's demand rather than holding his son responsible for his misdeeds. Not only did Absalom gain an audience with the king, but he was also allowed to return to Israel and to his life as if nothing had happened.

The Bible tells us that soon after this, Absalom started to conspire against his father. He went to the city gates every day and won the affections of the people. He blatantly told the people that his father could not be bothered with the ordinary issues people faced and offered himself as their advocate. More and more people followed Absalom and became disloyal to David. In time, Absalom had enough support from the military and the citizens of Israel to stage a coup.

David was forced to flee Israel with his wives, children and men who were still loyal to him. He left ten of his concubines in the castle to take care of his estate. Ahitophel's first advice to Absalom was to take these concubines and sleep with them on the rooftop of the castle for the whole nation to see. This was intended to be an ultimate act of profound disrespect. Public humiliation at its finest. Then, Ahitophel advised Absalom to pursue David while the group would be tired and worn out from running away. Ahitophel knew from experience how difficult it was to flee from an enemy when small children and women were part of the group.

Hushai shrewdly counteracted Ahitophel's advice to pursue David and overtake him while his camp was weary from traveling. Hushai suggested that David and his mighty men would be ready for such an assault and Absalom would lose his whole army if they fought on that day. Absalom listened to Hushai rather than to Ahitophel. In fact, if Absalom had followed Ahitophel's advice about pursuing David and his family at that time, David wouldn't have been able to withstand the assault. Absalom's bid for the throne could very well have been successful. When Absalom chose to listen to Hushai, Ahitophel knew that the coup would not succeed. He put his affairs in order, then committed suicide by hanging himself with a rope (2 Samuel 16.)

The roots of Ahitophel's defection to Absalom is found in David's murder of Uriah. Ammiel, also known as Eliam, was another member of "The Thirty." He was Ahitophel's son and Bathsheba's father. Imagine what Eliam must have experienced when his beloved daughter was seduced by his King. This seduction would result in the murder of his son-in-law, who was also his comrade in arms. King David conspired to kill Uriah and left Eliam's beloved daughter a widow. He had to watch his daughter grieve her husband even as the nation of Israel perceived Bathsheba as the whore that seduced the king. What a betrayal from the king they had served and protected at the risk of their own lives! David's choices had far reaching repercussions for Bathsheba's whole family. This trauma would cut deeply and rock the core of the whole tribe.

Bathsheba also had a brother named Machir. Machir must have

been very different from the other men in the family. While his grandfather, father, and brother-in-law were known for their military feats, Machir was acknowledged for his acts of compassion. Machir housed Mephibosheth, Jonathan's son, before David ever knew Mephibosheth existed (2 Samuel 9:3.) Machir also met David by the streams when he was fleeing from Absalom. He provided David and his men with provisions and refreshments for their flight (2 Samuel 17: 27-29.) He continued to support David through his many mistakes. Once we put the pieces of the story together, it's obvious Bathsheba's family was torn apart by David's actions.

Bathsheba came from a family of men who were extremely loyal to David. They were shrewd and mighty warriors who regularly risked their lives to establish and defend David's throne. Odds are great that David and Bathsheba knew each other long before their adulterous affair. David's affair with Bathsheba, followed by his murderous plot to kill Uriah, would have had a tremendous impact on how the rest of the Mighty Men viewed him. They were all part of the same team.

Imagine what these men had gone through together: risking their lives to protect one another, comrades in arms, and facing and surviving numerous life-threatening battles together. What David did must have sent shock waves through the whole army. The sense of betrayal would have been very personal for these men who had fought beside David long before he became King over Israel.

Male bonding among warriors at this level would have been intense. To risk breaking this bond over a woman would have been especially contemptible. But David took this a step further. He didn't just fight with his friend over a woman. He stole his friend's wife when he had a harem full of beautiful women. After he unintentionally impregnated his friend's wife, he used his power as king to assure that his friend would be killed in battle.

Uriah most likely knew of what happened between Bathsheba and the king. The structure of the palace, where the guards were posted, and the fact that David and Bathsheba used messengers to communicate makes it likely that there were many who were aware of the incident. Knowing human nature, those in the know probably gossiped.

66

Some who knew may have even been Uriah's friends, eager to tell him what had happened while he'd been at war. When David tried twice to convince Uriah to go home and lay with his wife, Uriah may have known that he was being manipulated and set up. Uriah didn't challenge the king. Both times, he simply refused to partake in pleasure his comrades were denied in the fields as they waged war for their King and nation. Uriah was an honorable man.

After David's sins were exposed, the company of the Mighty Men was divided. Some remained loyal to David while others defected and joined Absalom's rebellion. They never regained the sense of brotherhood and oneness that had existed before David's betrayal.

Meanwhile, David's children saw an example of their father committing atrocious sins against God, nation, and family. Lives were lost. Families divided. Communities destroyed. David's kingdom never fully recovered.

Grief and Reconciliation

How did Bathsheba view David? Did she go to David voluntarily? Or was she summoned by the king to his bed and not given a choice? Even if she voluntarily went to David, her feelings for Uriah had to have run deep. The Bible tells us that Bathsheba "mourned" for her husband when she learned of his death. The Hebrew word used here is "sapad", which means to "tear the hair and beat the breasts, to lament, to wail, to mourn."

She literally tore her hair and beat her breasts in grief. She had loved Uriah. Perhaps that's why when she is listed in Jesus' genealogy, she is not named in the original Greek Text. She is simply mentioned as "Uriah's wife." Maybe in her heart, Uriah had always remained her husband. Maybe God was honoring her love for Uriah by not claiming her as the wife of David. And maybe God was honoring an honorable man who had loyally served his king and his adopted country.

I wonder what Bathsheba felt when she was told that a prophet had come to pronounce the consequences of David's sins, which included the death of her unborn baby. What were her feelings toward David?

She had just lost her beloved husband due to her king's schemes. While in the throes of grieving her husband, she was rushed into marrying a king who already had multiple wives. She was no longer the beautiful and beloved bride of a man who adored only her. She had become another woman in a harem full of other beautiful women sharing the affections of one man. I doubt any of the women in David's harem welcomed her with gladness. Her whole life had been turned upside down. She had no family surrounding her and no friendly faces to talk to in the midst of profound grief. All she had were memories of a husband she'd betrayed and the baby in her womb conceived in adultery.

Maybe she'd resented the baby that had trapped her into these horrifying circumstances. Maybe she'd wished she had never conceived. What turmoil must have filled her heart? Grief-stricken and alone. Judged and hated. Isolated and abandoned. I don't think she felt like she could even turn to God for comfort. How could she when she was such a sinner? She didn't live in the age of Grace. She lived in the age of Law. The God of the Law was exacting and puni-tive. Adultery was punishable by death. I doubt she found comfort in this God.

If she had resented her pregnancy, what did she feel when she was told her baby would die? When she held her child for the first time, did she still fall in love with him, knowing he would not live? After she had nursed him for seven days, what was her grief like when she remembered how complicated her emotions had been about her baby?

I wonder how she and David reconciled enough to have another child. It's hard to imagine that Bathsheba would have easily welcomed him back into her heart. There must have been tears, accu-sations, many hurtful words before there was a reconciliation. The Bible tells us that "David comforted his wife Bathsheba, and he lay with her. She gave birth to a son, and they named him Solomon." Did part of David's "comfort" include confession, repentance, and a request for her forgiveness? A forgiveness that Bathsheba must have given.

The root of their second son's name is "shalom." It means peace. Peace between husband and wife. Peace, perhaps, between woman and God. And a hope that there would be peace in their household and their nation. The birth of Solomon was a new beginning for them all. (Psalm 51, David's psalm of repentance after the prophet Nathan confronted him with his sin, for a look inside David's heart at this time)

When Solomon was born, God sent Nathan, the prophet, to tell this trial-worn couple that He loved their son. He even gave them a new name for Solomon. God wanted to name him "Jedidiah" which meant "one beloved by YAHWEH." God was giving this couple comfort, restoration, and hope. Curiously enough, they didn't change their son's name. The name Solomon stuck. Perhaps, in the circumstances they were in, peace was more desirable than love.

Though David had numerous wives, he favored Bathsheba enough that they had four sons together. Also, it appears that some kind of a relationship sprang up between Nathan, the prophet, and Bathsheba because she named one of her sons after him. After Solomon's birth, there's a long lapse of many years before we read about Bathsheba again.

When we do, the prophet Nathan and Bathsheba are working together to establish Solomon's throne. It seems this prophet who initially stormed the palace, eager to pronounce God's judgment against David and Bathsheba, developed a soft spot for her and she for him. Nathan warned Bathsheba when Adonijah set himself up as King in anticipation of David's passing. And Nathan gave her the strategy that ultimately saved her life and established Solomon's kingdom. Somewhere along the way, the prophet and the adulteress had made peace.

Bathsheba learned about sin and its consequences the hardest way of all. Sin cost the lives of those she loved the most. Through these experiences, Bathsheba learned humility, wisdom and increased in faith. The Bible is clear that Bathsheba raised Solomon to revere God.

The Book of Proverbs is full of wise sayings that Solomon attributes to his mother. The Bible also tells us that Adonijah put himself forward to be King because, "His father had never challenged him by asking, "Why do you behave as you do?" (1 Kings 1:6) Apparently, David was not a father who taught his sons to love God as he did.

While some of David's other sons committed rape, murder, and staged coups against their father, one of the sons he had with Bathsheba strove to gain wisdom from God. He emerged as the heir to the throne above brothers who were older than him. It proved to be the right choice for Israel because, under Solomon's reign, the nation would attain a level of security, prosperity and peace never to be equaled again. Bathsheba also became the first woman of power in Israel's monarchy. She became the Queen Mother, the uncontested seat of power when no other woman before her had been honored in this way.

Something about her inspired such love and respect in Solomon that he placed a throne "at his right hand" for his mother to occupy. In fact, Solomon's first command as a king was to have a throne made for Bathsheba. This symbolically and practically presented her as the most powerful woman in the nation. This tradition of a Queen Mother co-ruling with the king would remain in Israel until Asa removed his mother from the throne (2 Chronicles 15:16). In a time when kings had multiple wives, rather than choosing one wife to co-rule, the kings of Israel followed Solomon's precedent and established their mother as the Queen. When the kings of Israel's stories are told, their mother's name and her genealogy are always listed to inform the readers who is co-ruling with the king.

After everything she had been through, this adulteress, a wife in low standing among many women who had married the king, emerged as the Queen. Solomon himself would marry many women, but none were given the title of Queen.

The Bible says that in his latter years, Solomon followed the gods of his wives and strayed from his devotion to YAHWEH. He allowed the gods of his many wives to be worshiped in the nation of Israel and committed idolatry. I tend to think that once Bathsheba died and

Solomon no longer had the wise counsel of his mother, he listened to his many wives and was led astray. Bathsheba helped to anchor her son's faith in the one true God and co-ruled with him to establish the way of YAHWEH in the chosen nation of Israel. Once Solomon lost his mother, he lost his anchor and was tempted by other gods.

The Queen and God's Mercy

Above all the women in David's life, Bathsheba was chosen to mother the Messianic line. In fact, she is represented on both sides of Jesus' lineage through her sons Solomon and Nathan. We can read accounts of other wives in David's life who seem so much more quali-fied. Abigail, Nabal's widow, comes to mind. Abigail showed prudence, generosity, and grace, which won her David's heart. He proposed to her as soon as her husband died and we never read anything negative about her afterward. Why was Bathsheba the chosen one to bear the Messianic line?

Maybe it's because Bathsheba learned a lesson about grace. Her life story also exhibits the beauty of God's grace and mercy. She was never deserving and never earned anything, but she lived through horrific life and death consequences of sin. Apparently, through her trials, she learned to fear God and raised a son fit to be King over a nation that God had set apart as His very own. God redeemed a rela-tionship that had its roots in adultery and murder.

We don't know if Bathsheba was a victim or an accomplice. What we do know is that through God's mercy, this union was blessed. The consequences of David's sin with Bathsheba and the murder of Uriah are so far-reaching, we can argue that the entire course of Israel's history was changed after these incidents. Who knows how many relationships were severed and how many lives destroyed as a result of this relationship?

Bathsheba married again. Bathsheba had more children. The outcast who was despised by those around her rose to be the Queen of God's chosen nation. Hers is a story of redemption and restoration; the very things that Jesus came to accomplish on earth. In the end, the message of this story is not that man's sin prevails. The message of this story is that in the midst of human wickedness, weakness and failure, God's mercy still triumphs.

Bathsheba is in Jesus' genealogy as a reminder to us that only God can reverse the effects of sin and make good come out of something bad.

From sinner to Royalty. From victim to Queen.

Going Deeper

1. Most likely, Bathsheba was not a willing participant when David forced himself on her. Have you ever been a victim of a crime? Have you forgiven those who have hurt you?

2. Bathsheba is still labeled an adulteress by many Christians. Have you experienced gossip and slander based on partial truths, outright lies, or distorted perceptions? How did you deal with these situations?

3. Have you willingly believed the worst about another person when you do not really know them? Have you spread gossip you've heard or started a rumor that could hurt someone?

4. Is there a situation you're still waiting for the vindication of the Lord?

5. Though David made crucial mistakes as a father, Bathsheba was a wonderful mother and counselor. If you're a parent, and your partner is not the best father/mother, how can you raise healthy children without turning them against the other parent?

Prayer of Blessing

Father, thank you for being the God of healing. You take our pain and turn it for our good. Bathsheba never wanted her husband to die or to join a harem. Yet, you saw her pain and elevated her as a queen. We know that you can promote us. You upgrade our experiences and bring about good results we could not have imagined. We are believing you for vindication, promotion, and restoration. In the areas where crime or injustice has not been fully resolved in our lives, we ask for your resolution. We are believing you for healing and closure. We will not agree with gossip, slander, and mistreatment of others. We repent for the times we have partnered with the accuser. We release your blessings over those we've hurt. We forgive those who have cursed us, betrayed us, or spread lies about us. We declare that you are the God who restores what was lost. Your ways are higher than our ways. All the areas of our lives the enemy has killed, stolen, or destroyed, we now declare to be a place abundant life will manifest. We are positioned for breakthrough and we thank you for the upgrades.

References:

2 Samuel 11:1-27

David and Bathsheba

Then it happened in the spring, at the time when kings go out *to battle*, that David sent Joab and his servants with him and all Israel, and they destroyed the sons of Ammon and besieged Rabbah. But David stayed at Jerusalem.

2 Now when evening came David arose from his bed and walked around on the roof of the king's house, and from the roof he saw a woman bathing; and the woman was very beautiful in appearance. 3 So David sent and inquired about the woman. And one said, "Is this not Bathsheba, the daughter of Eliam, the wife of Uriah the Hittite?" 4 David sent messengers and took her, and when she came to him, he lay with her; and when she had purified herself from her uncleanness, she returned to her house. 5 The woman conceived; and she sent and told David, and said, "I am pregnant."

6 Then David sent to Joab, *saying*, "Send me Uriah the Hittite." So Joab sent Uriah to David. 7 When Uriah came to him, David asked concerning the welfare of Joab and the people and the state of the war. 8 Then David said to Uriah, "Go down to your house, and wash your feet." And Uriah went out of the king's house, and a present from the king was sent out after him. 9 But Uriah slept at the door of the king's house with all the servants of his lord, and did not go down to his house. 10 Now when they told David, saying, "Uriah did not go

down to his house," David said to Uriah, "Have you not come from a journey? Why did you not go down to your house?" **11** Uriah said to David, "The ark and Israel and Judah are staying in temporary shelters, and my lord Joab and the servants of my lord are camping in the open field. Shall I then go to my house to eat and to drink and to lie with my wife? By your life and the life of your soul, I will not do this thing." **12** Then David said to Uriah, "Stay here today also, and tomorrow I will let you go." So Uriah remained in Jerusalem that day and the next. **13** Now David called him, and he ate and drank before him, and he made him drunk; and in the evening he went out to lie on his bed with his lord's servants, but he did not go down to his house.

14 Now in the morning David wrote a letter to Joab and sent *it* by the hand of Uriah. **15** He had written in the letter, saying, "Place Uriah in the front line of the fiercest battle and withdraw from him, so that he may be struck down and die." **16** So it was as Joab kept watch on the city, that he put Uriah at the place where he knew there *were* valiant men. **17** The men of the city went out and fought against Joab, and some of the people among David's servants fell; and Uriah the Hittite also died. **18** Then Joab sent and reported to David all the events of the war. **19** He charged the messenger, saying, "When you have finished telling all the events of the war to the king, **20** and if it happens that the king's wrath rises and he says to you, 'Why did you go so near to the city to fight? Did you not know that they would shoot from the wall? **21** Who struck down Abimelech the son of Jerubbesheth? Did not a woman throw an upper millstone on him from the wall so that he died at Thebez? Why did you go so near the wall?'—then you shall say, 'Your servant Uriah the Hittite is dead also.'"

22 So the messenger departed and came and reported to David all that Joab had sent him *to tell*. **23** The messenger said to David, "The men prevailed against us and came out against us in the field, but we pressed them as far as the entrance of the gate. **24** Moreover, the archers shot at your servants from the wall; so some of the king's servants are dead, and your servant Uriah the Hittite is also dead." **25** Then David said to the messenger, "Thus you shall say to Joab, 'Do not let this thing displease you, for the sword devours one as well as another; make your battle against the city stronger and overthrow it'; and *so* encourage him."

26 Now when the wife of Uriah heard that Uriah her husband was dead, she mourned for her husband. **27** When the *time of* mourning was over, David sent and brought her to his house and she became his wife; then she bore him a son. But the thing that David had done was evil in the sight of the Lord.

2 Samuel 12:1-25

Nathan Rebukes David

1 Then the Lord sent Nathan to David. And he came to him and said,

"There were two men in one city, the one rich and the other poor.

2 "The rich man had a great many flocks and herds.

3 "But the poor man had nothing except one little ewe lamb

Which he bought and nourished;

And it grew up together with him and his children.

It would eat of his bread and drink of his cup and lie in his bosom,

And was like a daughter to him.

4 "Now a traveler came to the rich man,

And he was unwilling to take from his own flock or his own herd,

To prepare for the wayfarer who had come to him;

Rather he took the poor man's ewe lamb and prepared it for the man who had come to him."

5 Then David's anger burned greatly against the man, and he said to Nathan, "As the Lord lives, surely the man who has done this deserves to die. **6** He must make restitution for the lamb fourfold, because he did this thing and had no compassion."

7 Nathan then said to David, "You are the man! Thus says the Lord God of Israel, 'It is I who anointed you king over Israel and it is I who delivered you from the hand of Saul. **8** I also gave you your master's house and your master's wives into your care, and I gave you the house of Israel and Judah; and if *that had been* too little, I would have added to you many more things like these! **9** Why have you despised the word of the Lord by doing evil in His sight? You have struck down Uriah the Hittite with the sword, have taken his wife to be your wife, and have killed him with the sword of the sons of Ammon. **10** Now therefore, the sword shall never depart from your house, because you have despised Me and have taken the wife of Uriah the Hittite to be your wife.' **11** Thus says the Lord, 'Behold, I will raise up evil against you from your own household; I will even take your wives before your eyes and give *them* to your companion, and he will lie with your wives in broad daylight. **12** Indeed you did it secretly, but I will do this thing before all Israel, and under the sun.'" **13** Then David said to Nathan, "I have sinned against the Lord." And Nathan said to David, "The Lord also has taken away your sin; you shall not die. **14** However, because by this deed you have given occasion to the enemies of the Lord to blaspheme, the child also that is born to you shall surely die." **15** So Nathan went to his house.

Loss of a Child

Then the Lord struck the child that Uriah's widow bore to David, so that he was *very* sick. **16** David therefore inquired of God for the child; and David fasted and went and lay all night on the ground. **17** The elders of his household stood beside him in order to raise him up from the ground, but he was unwilling and would not eat food with them. **18** Then it happened on the seventh day that the child died. And the servants of David were afraid to tell him that the child was dead, for they said, "Behold, while the child was *still* alive, we spoke to him and he did not listen to our voice. How then can we tell him that the child is dead, since he might do *himself* harm!" **19** But when David saw that his servants were whispering together, David perceived that the child was dead; so David said to his servants, "Is the child dead?" And they said, "He is dead." **20** So David arose from the ground, washed, anointed *himself*, and changed his clothes; and he came into the house of the Lord and worshiped. Then he came to his own house, and when he requested, they set food before him and he ate.

21 Then his servants said to him, "What is this thing that you have done? While the child was alive, you fasted and wept; but when the child died, you arose and ate food." **22** He said, "While the child was *still* alive, I fasted and wept; for I said, 'Who knows, the Lord may be gracious to me, that the child may live.' 23 But now he has died; why should I fast? Can I bring him back again? I will go to him, but he will not return to me."

24 Then David comforted his wife Bathsheba, and went in to her and lay with her; and she gave birth to a son, and he named him Solomon. Now the Lord loved him 25 and sent *word* through Nathan the prophet, and he named him Jedidiah for the Lord's sake.

1 Kings 1:5-31
Adonijah Sets Himself Up as King

5 Now Adonijah the son of Haggith exalted himself, saying, "I will be king." So he prepared for himself chariots and horsemen with fifty men to run before him. 6 His father had never crossed him at any time by asking, "Why have you done so?" And he was also a very handsome man, and he was born after Absalom. 7 He had conferred with Joab the son of Zeruiah and with Abiathar the priest; and following Adonijah they helped him. 8 But Zadok the priest, Benaiah the son of Jehoiada, Nathan the prophet, Shimei, Rei, and the mighty men who belonged to David, were not with Adonijah.

9 Adonijah sacrificed sheep and oxen and fatlings by the stone of Zoheleth, which is beside En-rogel; and he invited all his brothers, the king's sons, and all the men of Judah, the king's servants. 10 But he did not invite Nathan the prophet, Benaiah, the mighty men, and Solomon his brother.

Nathan and Bathsheba

11 Then Nathan spoke to Bathsheba the mother of Solomon, saying, "Have you not heard that Adonijah the son of Haggith has become king, and David our lord does not know *it*? 12 So now come, please let me give you counsel and save your life and the life of your son Solomon. 13 Go at once to King David and say to him, 'Have you not, my lord, O king, sworn to your maidservant, saying, "Surely Solomon your son shall be king after me, and he shall sit on my throne"? Why then has Adonijah become king?' 14 "Behold, while you

are still there speaking with the king, I will come in after you and confirm your words."

15 So Bathsheba went in to the king in the bedroom. Now the king was very old, and Abishag the Shunammite was ministering to the king. 16 Then Bathsheba bowed and prostrated herself before the king. And the king said, "What do you wish?" 17 She said to him, "My lord, you swore to your maidservant by the Lord your God, *saying*, 'Surely your son Solomon shall be king after me and he shall sit on my throne.' 18 Now, behold, Adonijah is king; and now, my lord the king, you do not know *it*. 19 He has sacrificed oxen and fatlings and sheep in abundance, and has invited all the sons of the king and Abiathar the priest and Joab the commander of the army, but he has not invited Solomon your servant. 20 As for you now, my lord the king, the eyes of all Israel are on you, to tell them who shall sit on the throne of my lord the king after him. 21 Otherwise it will come about, as soon as my lord the king sleeps with his fathers, that I and my son Solomon will be considered offenders."

22 Behold, while she was still speaking with the king, Nathan the prophet came in. 23 They told the king, saying, "Here is Nathan the prophet." And when he came in before the king, he prostrated himself before the king with his face to the ground. 24 Then Nathan said, "My lord the king, have you said, 'Adonijah shall be king after me, and he shall sit on my throne'? 25 For he has gone down today and has sacrificed oxen and fatlings and sheep in abundance, and has invited all the king's sons and the commanders of the army and Abiathar the priest, and behold, they are eating and drinking before him; and they say, '*Long* live King Adonijah!' 26 But me, *even* me your servant, and Zadok the priest and Benaiah the son of Jehoiada and your servant Solomon, he has not invited. 27 Has this thing been done by my lord the king, and you have not shown to your servants who should sit on the throne of my lord the king after him?"

David Makes Solomon King

28 Then King David said, "Call Bathsheba to me." And she came into the king's presence and stood before the king. 29 The king vowed and said, "As the Lord lives, who has redeemed my life from all

distress, **30** surely as I vowed to you by the Lord the God of Israel, saying, 'Your son Solomon shall be king after me, and he shall sit on my throne in my place'; I will indeed do so this day." **31** Then Bathsheba bowed with her face to the ground, and prostrated herself before the king and said, "May my lord King David live forever."

1 Chronicles 3:4-5

4 Six were born to him in Hebron, and there he reigned seven years and six months. And in Jerusalem he reigned thirty-three years. **5** These were born to him in Jerusalem: Shimea, Shobab, Nathan and Solomon, four, by Bath-shua the daughter of Ammiel;

Matthew 1:6

Jesse was the father of David the king. David was the father of Solomon by Bathsheba who had been the wife of Uriah.

Luke 3:31

the son of Melea, the son of Menna, the son of Mattatha, the son of Nathan, the son of David,

THE MOTHER

"Oh God, Lord of heavenly hosts, do something!" Mary had always known He had never belonged to her. But for His life to end like this...what could God be thinking? How could He allow this? Why would God send His own Son and let Him die like this? Why had He given her a mother's heart to love Him if He had known it would end this way?

Memories of His life flashed before her. His birth, His childhood, and the glorious day when His ministry had begun and the whole world could see that He was no ordinary man. How proud she had been and how anxiously she had waited for His glory to be revealed! How many miracles had He performed? Too many to count. And she had rejoiced when she heard about them. Some she had seen with her own eyes. Did the people not see who He was? Oh, how she loved Him.

Looking up, she saw the rivulets of blood stain the cross from the tip of her son's precious head. Even the wooden beams holding Jesus looked like spears jutting from the deep. Everything in this scene looked violent and cruel. The whole world could see Jesus being crucified like some evil criminal. Her hands were clasped under her chin, against her heart, as she inwardly begged God

Almighty to intervene and save His Son. Though she knew better, her heart whispered. "Please, God, please. Save Him. He is hurting. They've tortured Him, and He will die if you don't intervene. You're mighty. You're God. I know this is your Son. Do something! Please, do something! I don't understand. Why would He be born to die this way?"

She remembered the words of the prophet Simeon. His words had been ringing inside of her ever since they had come to tell her that Jesus had been arrested. Hadn't he prophesied, "A sword will pierce your soul?" Is this what he had meant?

"Dear woman," came the rasping, tortured voice of her precious firstborn. She looked up. He was gazing down at her, His eyes so gentle, so full of concern for her when He was the one hanging on the cross. She strained to be coherent as she answered him, but she couldn't. Her throat was completely swollen shut with sorrow. Tears fell from her eyes, and the dripping sound they made on her robe sounded like blood. She could only nod to let Him know she heard Him. Her entire being was at complete attention.

"Here is your son..." His gaze switched to John, who was standing beside her, drowning in his grief as much as she. Jesus blinked rapidly to keep the blood from dripping into His eyes. She glanced at John. He stared at Jesus while sobs rent his body. He was shaking and shuddering with grief. His refusal to move away from Jesus touched her. He loved her Son. How could she not love someone who loved her Son?

"Here is your mother," He commanded. Though it cost Him, Jesus nodded slightly toward her, and John understood. John vigorously nodded his head and moved closer to her, wrapping his arm around her shoulder like a son comforting his mother, and Mary turned into him. Their shared grief bound them. Their mutual desire was to ease His suffering as much as they could. Jesus sighed in relief as if He had taken care of something that was important to Him.

Hadn't He always been like this? Thinking of others' needs before His own. So different from the other children, so perfect in His ways, she'd never been able to forget that He was God clothed in flesh. Even still, she had raised Him, nurtured Him, fed Him, and prayed for Him. She couldn't help it. She was his mother.

Mothering God

Luke is the only one who gives us an account of Mary being summoned to bear the Son of God. Theologians agree that each gospel shares a different aspect of Jesus. The four perspectives comprise a perfect picture of Jesus as King, Servant, Man, and God. Luke's primary goal is revealing Jesus as completely man. Since Luke is interested in showing that Jesus was fully human, he includes the story of a mom who is preparing for the birth of her son. Luke wants to show us that Jesus had a human mother who prepared for His birth much like any other mother would. Of course, the prophecies and the angelic visitations mark Jesus to be completely unique. Nevertheless, Jesus, like other babies, had a mother who bore Him and celebrated His birth.

Mary never forgot that Jesus was God. From that first angelic visitation announcing that she would be overshadowed by the Spirit of the Most High God to the moment that Jesus ascended to heaven, Mary knew that Jesus was never really her son. She was simply the chosen servant to bear this most precious life.

Luke's gospel gives us glimpses of what it must have been like for Joseph and Mary to raise the Son of God. After the shepherds had come to worship the newly born Savior, Luke tells us that, "Mary treasured up all these things and pondered them in her heart." Eight days after Jesus was born, in accordance with the other Jewish boys, He was taken to the temple to be circumcised. Joseph and Mary met a prophet and a prophetess who recognized that Jesus was the Messiah they had been waiting for all these years. The first prophet, Simeon, uttered marvelous prophecies about Jesus and "the child's father and mother marveled at what was said about Him."

We gain another glimpse of Jesus as a twelve-year-old boy. He remained in the temple after the Passover Feast and His parents didn't realize that He'd been missing for a whole day. These young parents

WOMEN IN JESUS' LIFE

commenced a frantic search for their son. He was finally found in the temple after three days of frantic searching.

As a mother, this is the ultimate nightmare; losing your child. Imagine being Mary. She knew that Jesus was the Son of God. She knew the supernatural circumstances surrounding His birth. She lived with the awareness that she'd been given an incredible divine trust. Then she lost Him! I wonder what kind of prayers she uttered to God the Father. Apologies? Reminders that, after all, Jesus was His Son, so it would be in His best interest to keep Him safe? What were her thoughts, feelings, and state of mind? Wouldn't you like to know? I would. But, again, the Holy Spirit doesn't give us a whole lot of details. He simply relates the events as they unfold.

Interestingly, the Bible does give us a glimpse of how Mary must have related to Jesus. When He was finally found, she admonished Him.

"Son, why have you treated us like this? Your father and I have been anxiously searching for you."

Jesus answered, quite boldly for a twelve-year-old, "Why were you searching for me? Didn't you know I had to be in my Father's house?"

Mary didn't have a response. Perhaps, she'd been rendered speechless. Jesus had a way when mere human beings challenged Him. He had a habit of asking a question that defied answers. If that had been my son, he would have gotten an earful. "Yes, it's great you're about God's business, but not at the expense of your mother's sanity! At least not yet. Maybe when you're a full-grown man you can make those decisions. But not while I'm still responsible for raising you. Do you realize you've been missing for four days? Why weren't you looking for me? Next time, make sure you stay with the family!" That would be the natural response of any mother.

But Mary doesn't respond this way. She'd been firmly reminded that Jesus was no ordinary child. He was born for the purpose of dealing with His Father's business. And that Father was not Joseph.

I find her question interesting. "Why have you treated us like this?"

There's an assumption being made in her question that she is the recipient of Jesus' treatment. Not the other way around. Usually, healthy parents aren't as concerned about how their children treat them because their focus tends to be on how they treat their children. Parents generally focus on teaching, disciplining, and shaping our children's character. A healthy parent doesn't allow the children to set the standard for the family. Such an approach would raise narcissistic people. A healthy parent wouldn't decide methods of discipline based on the child's reactions. Such an approach would be highly selfish and cowardly.

I don't ask my children when they misbehave, "Why are you treating me like this?" That focus becomes my feelings, not proper character development of my child.

My response to them misbehaving would be, "Do you realize what you've done?" Then I'd dive into explaining the situation for them so they understood what happened. The purpose is to prevent such poor choices from happening again. The posture of most healthy parents, when dealing with their children, is not one of being a passive recipient. We respond to our children, especially in crisis situations, with an eagerness to teach, admonish, and discipline. Neither Joseph nor Mary responded like typical healthy parents. They deferred to Jesus. They asked, "Why did you treat us like this? We were so anxious."

Mary's question wasn't an indication of poor parenting. She'd come to a shocking realization that this child, who had never sinned, had just behaved completely contradictory to His normal character. She gave Him a chance to explain. Rather than jumping to conclusions and punishing Him for His behavior, Mary was treating Jesus with the respect and honor He'd earned through years of obedience, submission to authority, and perfect life choices. The Bible tells us that Jesus grew in favor with God and man. His favor increased because He made choices to honor God and honor the people around Him.

Mary must have remembered this moment for the rest of her life. It wasn't just the trauma of losing Him that marked her. It was the way He responded to the situation that marked this experience for her. The Bible says Mary "treasured all these things in her heart." Apparently so, since she related this story to Luke many years later.

The gospel of John also gives us precious glimpses into this most unusual Mother-Son dynamic. John's unique perspective is to present the fullness of Jesus' Divine nature. His account of Jesus' ministry is significantly different than the synoptic gospels and offers several stories about Jesus that we don't get from Matthew, Mark, and Luke.

John recorded Jesus' first miracle. It's noteworthy that His first miracle occurred because His mother had requested His help. More than likely, Mary was already a widow. She was used to leaning on her oldest son for help. And Jesus being Jesus had probably made it fairly easy for her to rely on Him.

Jesus was attending the wedding banquet with His new disciples. The wedding feast ran out of wine. Mary didn't know what to do, but she knew that her Son was resourceful as well as helpful. Mary went to Jesus and informed Him, "They have no more wine."

Jesus' answer puzzles us. He said, "Dear woman, why do you involve me? My time has not yet come." I would venture to guess that His answer didn't make a whole lot of sense to Mary either. The first part of His answer sounds very much like a rebuke. The more correct translation of what Jesus said would be, "Woman, what does this have to do with me and you?" The more correct translation sounds like He was being pushed into doing something that He'd rather not do.

The Significance of the Wedding Feast

I have a thought about Jesus' answer. If you'll follow this line of thinking with me, I'd like to share it. I think Jesus was being prophetic. I believe Jesus was saying that His time to wed, to claim His Bride, had not yet come. We know that the Bride of Christ refers to the Church. John tells us in the book of Revelation that when Jesus returns to earth for the second time, He is coming back as a Bridegroom to claim His Bride. He will unite with the Church and bring her home to heaven. Then there will be a huge wedding banquet in heaven. This will be a huge feast celebrating the much-anticipated union between Jesus and His Bride.

At the wedding in Cana, Jesus was awaiting the beginning of His

85

earthly ministry. He'd just gathered a small group of young disciples. He had yet to reveal the true nature of His mission and He could not think about enjoying a wedding banquet of His own until His mission on earth was accomplished. I think when Jesus was at the wedding in Cana, He was looking forward to the day when He would claim His own Bride. He knew what lay ahead and what He would need to go through before the church could even be established. I believe His answer wasn't so much resistance to helping his mother but the reflections of His own heart that longed for the wedding banquet to be His own. Yet, in that moment, Jesus knew such a time was far off in the future.

It seems Mary heard and saw something in His demeanor that gave her hope. Mary commanded the servants to do whatever He told them. We know that Jesus had every intention of turning water into wine at that wedding. It was another prophetic act. But that topic deserves its own book.

What is established in this story is that Jesus is not treating Mary as a son would treat his mother. He called her "Woman." Not "Mother." He redefined their relationship. Yet, Mary was not in any way offended because she still expressed full confidence in Him. She trusted Him to bring a solution in the midst of crisis. There was a consistent humility in the way she interacted with Him. She never treated Jesus as a normal mother would treat a normal son. These stories reveal that Mary never forgot that when she was dealing with Jesus, she was dealing with God Himself. She did not consider herself to be equal to Him. In the Biblical stories, Mary never expressed an authoritarian role in Jesus' life.

The Humility of a Mother

I doubt that Mary's humility diminished her love for Him in any way. She had the unique privilege of being the chosen Mother to God's own Son. She nurtured Him through infancy, raised Him through childhood, and supported Him in His ministry. She met His first disciples and attended a wedding feast with them. She watched as the whole town of Nazareth turned against Jesus because of what He boldly declared in the synagogue. She visited her son during His times of public ministry and at times was rebuffed when Jesus would say things like, "Who is my mother, and who are my brothers?" And she stood by Him during His death and crucifixion.

The one portrayal of Mary during the crucifixion of Christ is Jesus remembering His responsibilities as the eldest son and providing security for her. Her reaction isn't recorded because it doesn't need a description. She would have grieved as any mother would have grieved in that circumstance. She would have loved Him as only she could. She had a mother's love for the life she bore.

What amazes me is that, in the midst of such pain and turmoil, Jesus fulfilled His duty as the oldest son and made certain His mother was taken care of. I don't think Jesus was checking off a mental list of responsibilities. We're seeing the real Jesus exposed to the core during the most painful experience anyone could go through. When the soldiers nailed His hands and feet, He interceded for them, saying, "Father, forgive them, for they do not know what they are doing."

As He hung on the cross, bearing the guilt of a fallen world, His body brutally torn from flogging, His head crowned with thorns, His eyes landed on the woman who birthed Him. The only person in the world who could love Him as a Mother loves her son. And He remembered her. Her heartache meant something to Him even in those circumstances. He expressed His love and concern for her by making sure she knew her future would be secure. She was not abandoned. This is the Jesus Mary had always known, the Jesus she had seen from infancy and had loved with her whole heart.

Favor and Humility

The most striking characteristic of Mary is that she remained humble. She didn't boast about her special connection to Jesus. She never argued with Him or pretended to know more than Him because she was His mother. If we really think about this, there is no one else born on earth that has been given the kind of favor, honor, and trust that she'd been given by God. If anyone had the right to boast in anything spiritual, it would have been Mary. Surprisingly, she remained a quiet voice throughout the Scriptures. She blended in with the crowd that followed Jesus while anticipating the coming of the Holy Spirit in the book of Acts.

The gospel of John relates the story of Jesus' brothers practically accusing Him of being a glory-seeker and a fame-hound by our modern language (John 7:1-5.) They were not believers of Jesus nor did they support His ministry before the resurrection. I imagine Mary had plenty to say to them about their stubbornness. I would go so far as to say she was probably a very good mother to them and treated them as sons that needed the strong hand of guidance and maternal wisdom.

We know Jesus' brothers became some of Jesus' most faithful followers after His ascension to heaven. Two of Jesus' brothers contributed to the New Testament; the books of James and Jude. James is mentioned several times as the leading apostolic voice in the Early Church. In fact, tradition tells us that he spent so much time on his knees in prayer that his nickname was "camel knees." Of course, these brothers' faith was based on who Jesus was. However, I'd wager that Mary's guidance and testimony had a profound influence on them.

In the end, Mary's remarkable contribution isn't that she gave birth to the Son of God but that she didn't allow that distinction to trap her into the easiest sin for humanity to fall into: pride. She avoided taking credit for anything that God had done in her or through her. She didn't lay claim to Jesus' ministry in any way. All the stories written in the Bible about her are stories that reflect humility.

Mary never sought her own honor and glory. She was a safe person for God to entrust with the life of His Son. Mary was the mother because she refused to gain honor or distinction based on God's sovereignty. She simply submitted. How fitting is it that the one chosen to bear the Servant-King, who completely emptied Himself to come and rescue a fallen world, would, herself, be such a humble vessel?

. . .

Going Deeper

1. Some people are born with incredible privilege, gifts, talents, and anointing. Have you experienced such high favor from God? How did you keep from falling into pride?

2. Have you ever idolized a person because you saw extreme favor on their lives?

3. How can we steward the gifts of God without falling into pride? How can we also keep from falling into false humility?

4. How would you describe genuine humility?

Prayer of Blessing

Father, thank you that all your children are born with a measure of favor. Thank you that we are all given purpose, significance, and destiny. If there is any hidden pride that would take credit for the gifts you've given us, we ask for your forgiveness. If we have belittled your divine gifts in an effort to look humble, we ask for your forgiveness. We open our lives to you to be holy vessels of your Spirit. Even as Mary carried God in her womb, we thank you for allowing us to be carriers of your Holy Spirit. Teach us how to partner with your Spirit in us. We ask for you to have your way in us and through us. We gratefully receive your complete protection from the evil one that seeks to destroy us and our children. We declare that this is the season to birth divine destinies and we receive the provision and resources that are needed for our callings to be fulfilled. We believe that Jesus accomplished full victory at the cross and we're more than conquerors because of what He has done.

References:

Luke 1:26-38

The Birth of Jesus Foretold

26 Now in the sixth month the angel Gabriel was sent from God to

---

a city in Galilee called Nazareth, **27** to a virgin engaged to a man whose name was Joseph, of the descendants of David; and the virgin's name was Mary. **28** And coming in, he said to her, "Greetings, favored one! The Lord *is* with you." **29** But she was very perplexed at this statement, and kept pondering what kind of salutation this was. **30** The angel said to her, "Do not be afraid, Mary; for you have found favor with God. **31** And behold, you will conceive in your womb and bear a son, and you shall name Him Jesus. **32** He will be great and will be called the Son of the Most High; and the Lord God will give Him the throne of His father David; **33** and He will reign over the house of Jacob forever, and His kingdom will have no end." **34** Mary said to the angel, "How can this be, since I am a virgin?" **35** The angel answered and said to her, "The Holy Spirit will come upon you, and the power of the Most High will overshadow you; and for that reason the holy Child shall be called the Son of God. **36** And behold, even your relative Elizabeth has also conceived a son in her old age; and she who was called barren is now in her sixth month. **37** For nothing will be impossible with God." **38** And Mary said, "Behold, the bondslave of the Lord; may it be done to me according to your word." And the angel departed from her.

Luke 2:41-52
The Boy Jesus at the Temple

41 Now His parents went to Jerusalem every year at the Feast of the Passover. **42** And when He became twelve, they went up *there* according to the custom of the Feast; **43** and as they were returning, after spending the full number of days, the boy Jesus stayed behind in Jerusalem. But His parents were unaware of it, **44** but supposed Him to be in the caravan, and went a day's journey; and they *began* looking for Him among their relatives and acquaintances. **45** When they did not find Him, they returned to Jerusalem looking for Him. **46** Then, after three days they found Him in the temple, sitting in the midst of the teachers, both listening to them and asking them questions. **47** And all who heard Him were amazed at His understanding and His answers. **48** When they saw

Him, they were astonished; and His mother said to Him, "Son, why have You treated us this way? Behold, Your father and I have been anxiously looking for You." **49** And He said to them, "Why is it that you were looking for Me? Did you not know that I had to be in My Father's *house?*" **50** But they did not understand the statement which He had made to them. **51** And He went down with them and came to Nazareth, and He continued in subjection to them; and His mother treasured all *these* things in her heart. **52** And Jesus kept increasing in wisdom and stature, and in favor with God and men.

John 2:1-12

Jesus Changes Water into Wine

2 On the third day there was a wedding in Cana of Galilee, and the mother of Jesus was there; **2** and both Jesus and His disciples were invited to the wedding. **3** When the wine ran out, the mother of Jesus said to Him, "They have no wine." **4** And Jesus said to her, "Woman,what does that have to do with us? My hour has not yet come." **5** His mother said to the servants, "Whatever He says to you, do it." **6** Now there were six stone waterpots set there for the Jewish custom of purification, containing twenty or thirty gallons each. **7** Jesus said to them, "Fill the waterpots with water." So they filled them up to the brim. **8** And He said to them, "Draw *some* out now and take it to the headwaiter." So they took it *to him.* **9** When the headwaiter tasted the water which had become wine, and did not know where it came from (but the servants who had drawn the water knew), the headwaiter called the bridegroom, **10** and said to him, "Every man serves the good wine first, and when *the people* have drunk freely, *then he serves* the poorer *wine; but* you have kept the good wine until now." **11** This beginning of *His* signs Jesus did in Cana of Galilee, and manifested His glory, and His disciples believed in Him. **12** After this He went down to Capernaum, He and His mother and *His* brothers and His disciples; and they stayed there a few days.

THE EVANGELIST

$\mathscr{T}$he Samaritan woman couldn't move. She stood in shock staring at the man standing before her. What had he said? A minor commotion stirred behind her, but she was oblivious. Her heart had stopped before it beat again. It beat so fast she couldn't breathe. She dropped the jar in her hands, and the water splashed down her robe, but she barely noticed.

In a daze, she looked around and realized that a group of men was standing behind her in awkward silence. They glanced at her, took a furtive look at the man who'd spoken to her, and stared at the ground in silent shame. She embarrassed them. Not an unfamiliar experience. She seemed to have that effect on a lot of people, but not him. Bewildered, she looked back at the man. He was watching her, his gaze steady. He didn't pay any attention to the men who were awkwardly waiting for Him.

All the while, a gentle smile never left His face. He wasn't ashamed or embarrassed. He wasn't in any hurry to disengage from her. In fact, the look in his eyes seemed like...well...like...love. Like he loved her. Not as other men had loved her. Not as others had professed to love her. He saw through her, knew her, and he loved her. The real her.

Slowly, she took a few steps back. She shook her head in wonder.

Then a compulsion took over that she couldn't resist, and she whirled about to run back into town. Electric excitement and joy like she'd never experienced filled her with life and energy. She had to run as fast as she could. She had to tell somebody. She had to tell the whole world. She had met the Christ!

The Social Reject

When I read the account of the "Woman at the Well," I like to add the word "Samaritan." So, I read it as "The Samaritan Woman at the Well." Maybe I should even take it a step further and title this encounter, "The Adulterous Samaritan Woman at the Well." For us, in this day and age, this roughly translates to, "The Ultimate Social Pariah at the Well."

I imagine her as quite beautiful yet filled with emotional issues. This woman had looked for love in all the wrong places. I don't think she had a friend: a true friend. In that culture and time, when a woman's value was measured by the worth a man placed on her, even her family would have labeled and abandoned her. She had had too many broken marriages and had been cast aside one too many times.

Though she was no longer married, she was currently living with a man. Who knew how long this current flame would last? She was probably resigned to the fact that he would leave her, too. Then what would happen to her? Where would her security come from?

The Bible tells us that she was drawing water at high noon by herself. Other women would have come first thing in the morning to draw water for the day to avoid the heat of the sun. They would have greeted each other with warm affection, friendship, familiarity, with a sense of community bonding them. They would have asked about each other's families, given advice, swapped recipes, and told a few jokes. They would have enjoyed the cool morning weather and taken their time with their chores in order to spend more time in fellowship.

She'd probably tried to join them for a while and finally given up when the repeated rejections became too painful. Maybe they'd even been her friends once. Not anymore. Now, she preferred to face the heat of the noonday sun to carry the heavy water jars rather than face the painful social isolation. Robin Williams, the great comedian, is quoted as saying, "People say the worst feeling in the world is loneliness. That's not true. The worst feeling in the world is to be surrounded by people who make you feel alone." This was her daily reality. She was surrounded by a whole village of people who made her feel alone. She must have felt alone even in her own home because she was living with a man who refused to marry her.

Which marriage had destroyed her reputation? The third? The fourth? Somewhere along the way, she had become an outcast relegated to fetching water during the hottest time of the day, alone. I used to wonder, was she barren? Did she keep remarrying because, though the men loved her, she wasn't able to bear a child? Did she have no son to care for her in her older years? Did she have to rely on her fading beauty and practiced charms to entice a man to care for her? These questions rolled around my head as I read her story over and over again. I wondered if she was facing the prospect of selling her body if this live-in lover left her, too.

I have a painting of the woman at the well sitting at the feet of Jesus in my devotion room. It's not done very well. It's one of those mass-produced pieces of art you can find on eBay. Still, it's the first religious art I actually purchased for myself. I'm drawn to this woman who was considered all wrong in about every category that was important for the Jews. She was the wrong race. The wrong class. The wrong gender. The wrong kind of sinner. Maybe even the wrong age. Nothing qualified her to be worthy of anything good.

In my imagination, she met Jesus when she was at the end of her rope. I see her in despair, resigned to rejection, loneliness, and hopelessness. She was simply going through the motions of life and believed herself to be worthless. I imagine this because the Jesus I know is drawn to people like her.

She'd had five husbands, and one more man who wanted the benefits of marriage he could take from her while refusing to give her the same. Then Jesus entered her life. The seventh man. The perfect man.

Indeed, the perfect Bridegroom. He chose to reveal His true identity, that He was the Messiah, to an adulterous Gentile woman.

In case she would mistakenly believe that she had earned this awe-inspiring revelation by anything she'd said or done, Jesus firmly relieved her of that notion by revealing that He knew her darkest of secrets. He didn't allow her to hold onto any illusions of performance-driven approval. Why? Because it wasn't anything about her that qualified her. It was simply that He chose to qualify. It wasn't the revelation of His identity that was epic. It was the way in which He chose to introduce Himself as the Messiah that said as much about who He was as the statement that, "I who speak to you am He (Messiah, called Christ)."

The Religious Leader and The Adulterous Gentile Woman

Just a chapter earlier, Jesus had told a well-educated religious leader (the right race, the right class, the right sex; as "righteous" as they come) that he hadn't "come into the world to condemn the world but to save it" (John 3:17.) What better way to illustrate His love for the world than to woo a woman of the world who was at the bottom of the totem pole of life. She, who deserved condemnation, indeed, probably had lived in condemnation for most of her life, was instead given divine revelation. In these two separate declarations of His identity, we are given the full spectrum of humanity. From one who met all the qualifications to one who had not a single qualifying characteristic. Jesus came for them both and for everyone in between.

I find it interesting that Jesus spent seventeen verses explaining to Nicodemus who He was and why He'd come into the world. I'm glad He did because this passage holds that most favorite verse of all, "For God so loved the world, He gave His one and only Son that whoever believes in Him shall not perish but have eternal life (John 3:16.)"

We don't have a record of Nicodemus' reaction to this extraordinary encounter with Jesus. We don't know if he left the mountain in the dark of the night leaping, rejoicing, and proclaiming that He had found the Messiah. I don't think anyone reading the Scriptures imagines that's how Nicodemus reacted.

I think he left the mountain as quietly as he'd arrived, lost in thought, analyzing what Jesus had said. Maybe even trying to reconcile his hope for the Messiah who would be a conquering military hero coming to rescue them from Roman oppression to this humble Rabbi talking about love, light, and life. We know that Nicodemus later became a believer, but his first encounter with Jesus didn't result in evangelism.

The contrast between Jesus' conversation with Nicodemus and the woman at the well is striking. Jesus spent seventeen verses explaining His incarnation to the well-educated Pharisee. After such a powerful time of encounter and divine revelation, Nicodemus probably left the mountain still puzzled and uncertain. On the other hand, Jesus' conversation with the woman at the well involved supernatural exposure of personal sin and unconditional divine acceptance. Jesus simply said, "I am the Messiah."

In each of these stories, we see Jesus confronting their religious shields. He refused to remain in doctrinal discussions about religion when both of these radically different individuals preferred that level of connection. He pressed in for a more heartfelt encounter and captivated their affections. Jesus has a way of doing that. He doesn't allow us to hide behind religious rhetoric, doctrinal discussions, and theological musings. Jesus always goes after our hearts.

This woman at the well is our first recorded evangelist. She ran into town, forgetting her shame, and became the voice that would draw the entire city to see Jesus for themselves. Jesus has a way of doing that to us. He makes us forget our shame. In her joyous excitement, she even forgot she was a social outcast.

She could have been ignored, reviled, or rejected outright. In that moment of radical encounter with the love of Jesus, rejection from an entire community no longer mattered. She had to share this incredible love with people who should have been her enemies. They actually were her enemies. These people had made her life miserable. But not anymore. She had found the answer to all her hopes and dreams, and He stood outside Samaria by an ancient well.

Jesus' dialogue with this woman is the longest recorded conversation he had with any person. Think about that. The Holy Spirit recorded this one conversation in more detail than any other conversation Jesus had. This outcast was that worthy, that important, and that lovable to God. Jesus saw past the woman's history and reputation to her deepest fears, hurts, and longings.

As Jesus talked with this prodigal daughter, He drew her to Himself. And she was transformed. One encounter with Jesus was enough to completely transform her. Not only did she experience divine love, she felt worthy. Perhaps for the first time ever in her whole life. When she felt worthy, even her enemies deserved to be told the good news. Jesus had to be shared, and her whole community had to be saved.

When Jesus' disciples returned from gathering food, they were shocked to see Him talking publicly with a Samaritan woman. He didn't rebuke them for their prejudice. Instead, He described a compelling vision of fields that were white, ready for harvest. Of course, He wasn't giving them a lesson on farming. Jesus was talking about a harvest of humanity, people ready to be brought into His kingdom.

As soon as she heard the "words of life" from Jesus, the Samaritan woman felt compelled to share them. She immediately left her water jar and ran to tell the villagers about her encounter with the Living Water. Through her testimony, she sowed spiritual seeds that yielded a great harvest that manifested when Philip, the deacon, went to Samaria after the ascension of Jesus. (Acts 8:5-25)

Equal to the Apostles

The Orthodox Church named the woman at the well as Photini, meaning "equal to the apostles." Tradition says that after Jesus' death Photini was baptized and traveled to many regions to preach the good news about her Savior. She and her children—five daughters and two sons—were arrested and taken to Rome. While in Rome, it's recorded that Photini witnessed to Nero's daughter, who became a believer. Eventually, Photini's entire family were martyred."

Jesus didn't really explain anything to her. When she referred to the coming Messiah, He said, "I who speak to you am He." Actually, in the original text, He said, "I AM." He proclaimed that He was the Great I AM, YAHWEH. She needed no further explanations. By the time Jesus declared His identity, Photini already knew He was no ordinary man. She already believed Him to be greater than anyone else she'd ever met. He had broken every cultural and religious standard to hold a lengthy public conversation with her. He was not ashamed nor was He afraid. Jesus took His time and cared for her heart even as He bluntly challenged her defenses. He stripped away her emotional games, named her sins, identified her issues with rejection yet remained deeply interested in her. He gifted her with divine revelation and treated her as a trusted friend before she had done anything trustworthy.

This encounter with God was not one of intellect but of the heart. Something in the way He revealed her past must have communicated such love and compassion that she felt no condemnation. She felt drawn to this man who regarded her with such value she was instantly transformed to one who boldly faced a hostile crowd without any fear. He revealed Himself to her at such a deep level, she instantly discovered what she was born for. Rejection and sin no longer defined her. She was healed. She was delivered. She was now an evangelist.

Such radical transformation overcame her that she went from being a social reject to one who the leaders of the early church called "equal to the apostles." A Samaritan. A woman. An adulteress. She had no social standing, no wealth, no education, and no credibility to mark her as a church leader. She had one thing that qualified her: her encounter with Jesus.

In this encounter, she believed Him to be who He said He was. In this belief, Photini found her destiny. She lived out this belief by testifying to the world about Jesus. In her testimony of Jesus, she found eternal purpose that defied the tortures and persecutions of the world. This encounter with Jesus was worth everything to her and when this testimony required her life, she gave it up gladly. Photini the evangelist also became Photini the martyr.

Her life displays that it only takes one true encounter with the love of Jesus to heal us and call out our true identity. In God's plan, this rejected social pariah had always been destined to be the first evangelist for Jesus.

Going Deeper

1. Have you ever felt rejection from a community? If you have, how did you overcome that? Identify any areas that still need healing.

2. Have you felt disqualified from your God-ordained purpose? Do you struggle with feelings of inferiority?

3. Nicodemus had all the right qualifications. Pharisees like Nicodemus often struggled with performance-driven identity. Do you have tendencies to base your worth on performance?

4. If you had no fear and all the resources in the world, what would be the one thing you really want to do with your life?

Prayer of Blessing

Father, thank you that your love is never based on what we do. Thank you for your unconditional love that gives us value, worth and joy. We invite your love and your healing. Free us from any performance-driven identity. Free us from regrets of the past. We receive your healing deliverance from any spirit of rejection, isolation, and depression. We will not partner with fear and shame. We rebuke the enemy's plans to isolate us and render us powerless, voiceless, and spineless. We declare our God-given identity that we are the Beloved. We believe for a bright future filled with purpose, passion, and power. Your love qualifies us to be bold and courageous. We gladly align with your truth. We will bring in the harvest and raise up more laborers out of our love for you. We will live in health and become change agents to create healthy communities. We will live out the purposes and plans you've had for us since the beginning of time. We wholeheartedly say yes to your commission.

References:
http://www.orthodoxchristian.info/pages/photini.htm

John 4:1-42

Jesus Talks With a Samaritan Woman

1 Therefore when the Lord knew that the Pharisees had heard that Jesus was making and baptizing more disciples than John 2 (although Jesus Himself was not baptizing, but His disciples were), 3 He left Judea and went away again into Galilee. 4 And He had to pass through Samaria. 5 So He came to a city of Samaria called Sychar, near the parcel of ground that Jacob gave to his son Joseph; 6 and Jacob's well was there. So Jesus, being wearied from His journey, was sitting thus by the well. It was about the sixth hour.

The Woman of Samaria

7 There came a woman of Samaria to draw water. Jesus said to her, "Give Me a drink." 8 For His disciples had gone away into the city to buy food. 9 Therefore the Samaritan woman said to Him, "How is it that You, being a Jew, ask me for a drink since I am a Samaritan woman?" (For Jews have no dealings with Samaritans.) 10 Jesus answered and said to her, "If you knew the gift of God, and who it is who says to you, 'Give Me a drink,' you would have asked Him, and He would have given you living water." 11 She said to Him, "Sir, You have nothing to draw with and the well is deep; where then do You get that living water? 12 You are not greater than our father Jacob, are You, who gave us the well, and drank of it himself and his sons and his cattle?" 13 Jesus answered and said to her, "Everyone who drinks of this water will thirst again; 14 but whoever drinks of the water that I will give him shall never thirst; but the water that I will give him will become in him a well of water springing up to eternal life."

15 The woman said to Him, "Sir, give me this water, so I will not be thirsty nor come all the way here to draw." 16 He said to her, "Go,

call your husband and come here." 17 The woman answered and said, "I have no husband." Jesus said to her, "You have correctly said, 'I have no husband'; 18 for you have had five husbands, and the one whom you now have is not your husband; this you have said truly." 19 The woman said to Him, "Sir, I perceive that You are a prophet. 20 Our fathers worshiped in this mountain, and you *people* say that in Jerusalem is the place where men ought to worship." 21 Jesus said to her, "Woman, believe Me, an hour is coming when neither in this mountain nor in Jerusalem will you worship the Father. 22 You worship what you do not know; we worship what we know, for salvation is from the Jews. 23 But an hour is coming, and now is, when the true worshipers will worship the Father in spirit and truth; for such people the Father seeks to be His worshipers. 24 God is spirit, and those who worship Him must worship in spirit and truth." 25 The woman said to Him, "I know that Messiah is coming (He who is called Christ); when that One comes, He will declare all things to us." 26 Jesus said to her, "I who speak to you am *He.*"

27 At this point His disciples came, and they were amazed that He had been speaking with a woman, yet no one said, "What do You seek?" or, "Why do You speak with her?" 28 So the woman left her waterpot, and went into the city and said to the men, 29 "Come, see a man who told me all the things that I *have* done; this is not the Christ, is it?" 30 They went out of the city, and were coming to Him.

31 Meanwhile the disciples were urging Him, saying, "Rabbi, eat." 32 But He said to them, "I have food to eat that you do not know about." 33 So the disciples were saying to one another, "No one brought Him *anything* to eat, did he?" 34 Jesus said to them, "My food is to do the will of Him who sent Me and to accomplish His work. 35 Do you not say, 'There are yet four months, and *then* comes the harvest'? Behold, I say to you, lift up your eyes and look on the fields, that they are white for harvest. 36 Already he who reaps is receiving wages and is gathering fruit for life eternal; so that he who sows and he who reaps may rejoice together. 37 For in this *case* the saying is true, 'One sows and another reaps.' 38 I sent you to reap that

for which you have not labored; others have labored and you have entered into their labor."

The Samaritans

39 From that city many of the Samaritans believed in Him because of the word of the woman who testified, "He told me all the things that I *have* done." 40 So when the Samaritans came to Jesus, they were asking Him to stay with them; and He stayed there two days. 41 Many more believed because of His word; 42 and they were saying to the woman, "It is no longer because of what you said that we believe, for we have heard for ourselves and know that this One is indeed the Savior of the world."

THE HONORED

I must find him!

The Canaanite woman knew she was getting close as she followed the horde of people. The nearer she got, the more urgent her need grew. She quickened her pace, keeping her head down as she wove through the crowd, and forced herself to the front of the gathering.

The mass stopped in front of a house because no one could enter. The door was closed to the public who were calling for Jesus. She dared to move a little closer, then knocked on the door. She cried out, "Lord, Son of David, have mercy on me! My daughter is suffering terribly!" She repeated herself while knocking, but no one answered. She was just another voice in the chanting mob, and she realized no one inside would pay her any attention. Someone shouted at her to be quiet and to wait her turn.

The opposition from the throng caused her to be even more determined. She had to find a way into the house. Jesus was in there. He could heal her daughter. She walked around to the back and saw servants running in with water and food. She snuck into the house posing as a servant. Once inside, she found her way to the living area. A small group of men was seated around a table, obviously waiting to be served their meal. She scanned the room with frantic eyes, her gaze roving until they landed on a man who was quietly listening to the conversation around him. His demeanor stood out to her. She studied him for a moment before deciding he was the one she had come to find.

Just then, as if he sensed her scrutiny, he looked at her across the room. Someone was eagerly telling him a story. He nodded to indicate that he had heard, but the focus with which he looked at her startled her. What was it about him? His piercing gaze made her feel like he already knew her. There was a warmth that took her by surprise, almost an invitation. His gaze broke away, and he glanced back at his companion.

If she had doubted the wisdom of what she was doing, it now dissipated, and her resolution grew stronger. With a clear purpose, she walked around the room. Servants were bustling around her, setting bread and wine on the table. She knelt beside his feet and said softly, "Lord, Son of David, have mercy on me. My daughter is suffering terribly from demon-possession."

Jesus continued listening to the man beside him and didn't even glance at the Canaanite woman. It stung. She thought about rising to leave. But the thought of her little girl in torment glued her to the spot. She glanced at his face. His gaze looked over her head. He didn't pay any attention to her, but she knew he could hear her. She needed to catch his attention quickly before she was thrown out.

A little louder this time, and with a sense of urgency, she said again, "Lord, Son of David, have mercy on me." She waited for him to answer, but he didn't. Someone made a shushing sound to her as if she was a nuisance. She ignored him. The only person she wanted to talk to was Jesus. "Lord," she said, a little louder this time, "Lord, Son of David, have mercy on me for my daughter is suffering terribly from demon-possession."

A man came to Jesus' side and said quite loudly, "Send her away, for she keeps crying out after us." Jesus finally looked at her. Again, his gaze was filled with unexpected knowledge and warmth. He studied her for a moment. Then he said, "I was sent only to the lost sheep of

Israel." Though the words were not encouraging, the tone of his voice was so warm, her heart filled with hope. She bowed her head before him. "Lord," she cried out, "help me!"

"It is not right to take the children's bread and toss it to their dogs."

His words struck her heart. The room grew quiet. The crowd had heard him, and the men were openly staring at her. She closed her eyes in shame and pictured her daughter. Even now, her daughter was lying in torment as wicked demons harassed her. Tears filled her eyes. When she opened them, rivers of sorrow stained her cheeks. Absorbing the pain of his words, she looked at him again with her heart full of pleading. Jesus had been watching her, and she felt waves of compassion emanating from him. He was so focused on her, and his gaze penetrated deep into her soul. In that moment, it felt like there was no one else in the room. It was just Jesus and her.

The tight knot of pain in her heart melted a little. She searched his countenance and saw only kindness. His words were at odds with the compassion in his eyes. More tears gathered and fell down her face as her heart throbbed with a mixture of pain and hope. Then she did the unthinkable. She touched him. She grabbed his hands and stared into his eyes even though tears blurred her vision. Swallowing the lump in her throat, her voice trembling with humility and emotion, she replied, "Yes, Lord. But even the dogs eat the crumbs that fall from their master's table."

Jesus' eyes shone with paternal pride, and He smiled. The warmth of it touched her to the core. "Woman, you have great faith!"

He paused and continued to beam at her with such pleasure, she couldn't help but smile back. Heaviness lifted from her heart, and she felt lighter. Hope filled her again. As she looked into his eyes, a strange, incomprehensible sense of joy spread through her heart. His presence healed a wounded and broken place inside of her. Somehow, he was intentionally washing away all sense of fear and rejection with his love. He leaned down so his eyes were level with hers. Their gazes locked. Tenderly, he said, "For such a reply, you may go; your request has been granted. The demon has left your daughter."

Her heart surged over with ecstasy. She knew he spoke the truth!

Even now, her daughter was free! With a joyous cry, she squeezed his hands to express her gratitude. Then she jumped up to run home. Her daughter was free!

A Desperate Mother's Hope

The story of the Canaanite Woman remains a challenge for most Christians. I don't know how many sermons I've heard on this story, but most of them struggled to explain Jesus' initial response. It's so unlike Him to be unkind, to respond harshly to someone's request for help. I struggled with that, too, for most of my life. The faith of this Canaanite woman astounded Jesus so much that her story is recorded in two of the gospels. Though her faith is remarkable, the true mystery of the story is Jesus' response.

Is there any valid reason that would justify how He demeaned her? In any culture, any setting, any time, isn't it truly demeaning to be likened to a dog? Some say He really called her a "puppy." Personally, I don't think I'd like to be called a puppy any more than a dog. It's no less dehumanizing.

I've heard preachers say it's because Jesus already knew how she would respond. Jesus wanted her faith to be revealed during testing. Then not only would God be glorified, but the Canaanite woman would also be eternally remembered. Other preachers have taught that Jesus was emphasizing He'd come for the Israelites first, and Christians should never forget that. Still others said it was to contrast the faith of a Gentile against the Israelites who refused to believe when the Jews should have been the first to receive Him.

It was quite confusing for me when I heard such different sermons on the same story. Eventually, I concluded it was mostly conjecture because the Bible doesn't explain what was really happening. Then I heard a sermon from Pastor Joseph Prince.

The revelation he received best explains Jesus' response. Pastor Prince explained that the title the Canaanite Woman was using for Jesus was an explicitly Jewish term. The phrase, "Son of David," was not a phrase other cultures used in reference to the Jewish Messiah.

Not even the Samaritans called the coming Messiah "Son of David." In fact, when we read Jesus' encounter with the Samaritan woman at the well, she said, "I know that Messiah, called Christ, is coming. When He comes, He will explain everything to us." (John 4:25) The Samaritan woman didn't call the Messiah "Son of David."

When the Canaanite woman approached Jesus with these words, "Lord, Son of David, have mercy on me," she was attempting to pass herself off as an Israelite. As a Gentile, she may have been afraid that Jesus would refuse her because she was not Jewish. She made a decision to approach Jesus deceptively. The desperation in her heart for her daughter was great. She was willing to go to any lengths for her daughter to be healed. Rather than risking rejection because of her ethnicity, her scheme was to deceive Jesus and manipulate him into healing her daughter. She called Jesus by a title that proved she believed Him to be the Messiah. But it was a title that was used exclusively by the Jews.

Jesus refused to play her game. When He responded with, "I was sent only to the lost sheep of Israel," He was giving her a chance to come clean. He let her know that He was not fooled and He knew she was not an Israelite. Rather than confessing and dealing with Jesus honestly, she threw herself at His mercy and pleaded, "Lord, help me." This ploy was a deliberate effort to play on His sympathies. In short, she was trying to manipulate Him. Jesus then challenged her and said the words that sounded so cruel. He said, "It is not right to take the children's bread and toss it to their dogs."

The gauntlet was thrown. He used the derogatory name that the Jews used to call her people, the Canaanites. He was telling her that He would not help her under these pretenses. Now the test was how she would respond. Offended? Hurt? Perhaps even denial and insistence on the pretense of being a Jew out of fear that she would be rejected.

This is where her heart was revealed. She knew she'd been exposed. There was no way to fool Jesus into believing that she was a Jew. Nevertheless, she persevered in faith. She wanted her daughter healed, and she knew He was the One who could help. She swallowed her pride, humbled herself, and spoke out in faith. She responded with the words made famous the world over: "Yes, Lord, but even the dogs eat the crumbs that fall from their masters' table."

It's interesting to note that the word for "Master" is in the plural; "masters." She was agreeing with Jesus that she was a dog. Jews were the masters, and she and her kind were dogs. If Jesus wanted to call her a dog, He could. She did not care. What she wanted was His healing touch on her daughter because she believed that He could do the miraculous. It wasn't about who she was. It was about who He was. She needed Him, and she would take Him on whatever terms He determined. She was desperate. Yet, it wasn't blind desperation. She was stating that she knew in Whom she believed.

As the Healer and Deliverer, Jesus had the right to identify and label people in whatever way He chose. Rather than taking offense and arguing with Him, the Canaanite woman humbled herself to Jesus' assessment. For this response, Jesus commended, "Woman, you have great faith." I don't think Jesus made this statement with some impassive objectivity devoid of emotion. Though Matthew and Mark both tell us this story, neither really gives us an emotional context for this scene.

I think He was so delighted with her He couldn't hide it. I think He was over the moon with her answer. Have you noticed that the Bible is woefully minimalistic about the stories it tells? Scripture usually gives us only the basic dialogue. It's almost like the Holy Spirit is inviting us to use our imagination to feel what these people went through. In different seasons of our lives, the same stories can convey a whole different feeling. I believe that the Lord did this on purpose so that the power of these testimonies would range much broader than if the emotions of the story were reported to us.

When I read the stories of people encountering Jesus, I like to close my eyes and imagine the scene before me. I ask the Holy Spirit questions, and I begin to see the humanity and the divinity of the story unfold like a movie. The Bible comes alive, and I realize that I can have the same kind of encounters with Jesus. And the feel of these stories change as the seasons shift in my life.

· · ·

Faith That Responds

The story of the Canaanite woman leaves much to the imagination. However, the one thing we cannot ignore is that the faith of this woman so impressed Jesus that He marveled and delighted in her. The Bible tells us repeatedly that God delights in faith. Hebrews 11:6 tells us, "Without faith, it is impossible to please God." What we know of God is that His greatest delight, His greatest pleasure, is in the faith of His children. This Canaanite woman displayed the best kind of faith. The kind that combines faith with true humility.

What we learn in this story is that Jesus does not play pretend. He will not have any part in schemes that employ deception. His heart always desires to heal and deliver, but He will not do so on false pretenses. Sometimes, when He calls us out on our "stuff", it can hurt. Sometimes, when we insist on pretense, we're met with silence and we think we're being ignored, rejected, or neglected. Sometimes, we may really believe that what we're presenting is the real deal. But He will insist on the truth.

When Jesus comes to the table, He waits until all the cards are displayed and the real, authentic, genuine matters of our hearts are revealed. He will persist in challenging us until we finally come to the place of gritty, brutal honesty. No matter how much it hurts, are we at the place of trusting Him enough to say, "I will always agree with what you call me. My identity is based on your assessment of me. If you call me a dog, then that's what I am. I will trust you because I know that without you, I have no hope. You are the answer I've been looking for my entire life."

The story of the Canaanite woman brings to mind the story of the woman who came to Jesus to touch the hem of His robe. In secret, she wanted to receive her healing. And in secret, she wanted to slip away. She believed that just touching the hem of His robe would heal her of a disease that had plagued her for twelve years. She wanted it without anyone else knowing about her needs, especially Jesus. But Jesus refused those terms. Jesus called attention to her and drew attention to her faith and her miracle.

The source of shame and embarrassment that had kept her

isolated and alone now became the source of public honor and intimate connection. The disease that drove her to Jesus, in secret desperation, became the place of her redemption. When she touched the hem of His robe with complete faith that He had the power to heal her, she did so anonymously. Jesus removed her veil of shame and replaced it with public acknowledgment of her incredible act.

When He drew attention to her and commended her for her faith, He essentially created an immediate community for her. The issue of constant bleeding made her unclean in the eyes of Mosaic law. She would have been socially isolated for the twelve years she had suffered from this disease. After the miracle, the whole community would know that she was now clean and whole. She was no longer unclean.

I imagine that many people thronged around her to ask what had just happened. How did she know that touching the hem of His robe would heal her? People would have been curious about her story. Thereby, this once lonely, rejected and religiously condemned woman would have been completely reinstated to society. Jesus offered this woman emotional, social, and spiritual healing to go along with her physical healing. He made her whole. And He personally connected to her on an intimate level by commending her faith. She felt seen and accepted by the most popular rabbi of the day. In one moment, her life was completely turned around. This single event restored everything this woman had lost. Just one healing encounter can do that for anyone. Jesus is that good!

Mark 6 records that many people sought to touch the hem of His garment to be healed. These "many people" had probably heard this woman's story of faith and healing. She had set a precedent many would follow to receive their miracle. If Jesus hadn't called attention to her courageous act of faith, others would have missed out on their healing miracle. This is the power of testimony. Jesus gave this lonely woman a platform of influence that allowed many others to also be healed.

Jesus doesn't want anyone sneaking in to get something from Him and then sneaking away after receiving the answer. He wants a relationship. Sometimes, He'll give you the healing first and He'll grant you the fulfillment of your hope. However, He wants to acknowledge you. He wants to say He's so glad you came to Him in faith.

Relating to Jesus is done on His terms. Why? Because His terms are clean, honest, and real. We are prone to games, secrets, shame, pride, guilt, and entitlement. But when He is in charge and He sets the terms, it's about being brutally honest, genuinely authentic, and stripping bare to the most vulnerable places. He insists on it. When He can reach that place, and we still trust Him and proclaim Him as our Lord, He honors us by commending our faith. He calls us His Beloved, and He announces to all creation that we stand in favor with Him.

The Canaanite woman received more than healing for her daughter that day. Jesus performed heart surgery on her and exposed her in the most vulnerable places. Emotionally, He stripped her bare and insisted on honesty. For the display of her genuinely humble faith in the midst of His challenge, she received a commendation that only one other person in the gospels received.

Jesus called her a person of great faith. She received His honor. To this day, wherever the gospel is preached, her faith is also preached. She also received a gift of revelation that took His disciples many more years to learn. Jesus is not a respecter of people, status, gender, ethnicity, or race. She received the revelation that Jesus is a respecter of faith.

Going Deeper

1. Can you think of a time you were being less than honest about your own motives to get what you want? Do you have a situation you're facing now where you need to get more honest with God?

2. Are you dealing with isolation or loneliness? What are some ways you can change this situation in church or other communities that matter to you?

3. Have you ever experienced a healing or deliverance miracle? If so, share it with a friend. If you're alone, take some time to meditate, remember, and give thanks to the Lord.

4. Do you currently have a healing or a deliverance need? Do you

have a loved one who needs a healing miracle? Take some time to pray for your healing. If you're with others in Bible study or prayer, ask for prayer.

Prayer of Blessing

Father, thank you for miracles, promises of healing, and deliverance that sets us free. We believe that you are the God of miracles and Jesus still heals today. We know that there's no power or authority that can set itself up against your children that is greater and stronger than you. We are your children, hidden and covered in the shadow of your wings. We claim Psalm 91 protection and blessing over ourselves and our loved ones. We believe in your promises that no disease, plague, destruction or powers of the enemy can harm us. You promised to satisfy us with a long life even as you rescue us from all harm because we love you and call on your name. We claim the name of Jesus. The blood of Jesus sets us free and the power of resurrection life lives inside of us. We rebuke every demonic spirit of disease, infirmity, affliction, harassment, and torment to leave our household now! We release the Holy Spirit and the angelic hosts over our homes and receive the freedom of Jesus Christ. We declare our homes, bodies, souls, and finances to be free of all anti-Christ influence. We demand the enemy to return to us seven-fold restoration of everything he's ever taken from us in time, energy, relationships, finances, and opportunities. We claim our plunder for every battle that's ever been waged against us. We declare the abundant life that Jesus declared and we agree with your will for our lives. We declare that we are the highly favored and the blessed.

References:

Matthew 15:21-28

The Faith of a Canaanite Woman

21 Jesus went away from there, and withdrew into the district of Tyre and Sidon. 22 And a Canaanite woman from that region came out and *began* to cry out, saying, "Have mercy on me, Lord, Son of

David; my daughter is cruelly demon-possessed." **23** But He did not answer her a word. And His disciples came and implored Him, saying, "Send her away, because she keeps shouting at us." **24** But He answered and said, "I was sent only to the lost sheep of the house of Israel." **25** But she came and *began* to bow down before Him, saying, "Lord, help me!" **26** And He answered and said, "It is not good to take the children's bread and throw it to the dogs." **27** But she said, "Yes, Lord; but even the dogs feed on the crumbs which fall from their masters' table." **28** Then Jesus said to her, "O woman, your faith is great; it shall be done for you as you wish." And her daughter was healed at once.

Mark 7:24-29

Jesus Honors a Syrophoenician
Woman's Faith

24 Jesus got up and went away from there to the region of Tyre. And when He had entered a house, He wanted no one to know *of it*; yet He could not escape notice. **25** But after hearing of Him, a woman whose little daughter had an unclean spirit immediately came and fell at His feet. **26** Now the woman was a Gentile, of the Syrophoenician race. And she kept asking Him to cast the demon out of her daughter. **27** And He was saying to her, "Let the children be satisfied first, for it is not good to take the children's bread and throw it to the dogs." **28** But she answered and said to Him, "Yes, Lord, *but* even the dogs under the table feed on the children's crumbs." **29** And He said to her, "Because of this answer go; the demon has gone out of your daughter."

THE DELIVERED

*D*arkness still reigned. The sun wouldn't rise for another couple of hours, but Mary was awake packing her precious bundle of oil and spices. She hadn't slept all night. She had tossed and turned fitfully, unable to erase the horrific images from her mind. Tears and sobs had mingled with outcries to Abba.

Hadn't He taught her to call God "Abba"? *Oh, Abba, where are you?* Her heart cried out in anguish. *I know what I've seen. I know what I was until Jesus delivered me. I know it was real. What are you doing? Where are you hiding? Did you not see what they did to Him? Your Son?*

A knock at the door broke the heavy silence in her home. "Mary? Are you up?"

Relief and warmth flooded through her. "Salome! I'm coming!"

She joined the group of women outside, each carrying their own bundles of perfumed oil and spices. Her friends. They embraced and tears flowed like a river. In the company of others who had loved Jesus as much as she had, there was no need to hold back her grief. They exchanged inquiries about each other's welfare and murmured about how unbelievable all this was.

The group realized that time was running out. It would soon be daybreak. They headed toward the tomb. They remembered where Joseph had taken Jesus' body.

"Who will roll the stone away from the entrance of the tomb?" Joanna asked.

None knew the answer. Maybe they could ask the Roman soldiers guarding the tomb to help them. Surely, they would be allowed to anoint His body.

They approached the tomb and looked up. The stone was already rolled away! They could make out the dark opening and the outline of the large stone against the hillside in the bright moonlight. Someone had already gone ahead of them. They rushed up the hill.

"Who do you think is here? Would His mother have come to anoint Him? Have you talked to her?" Mary asked the other Mary, Jesus' aunt.

"No," Mary, the aunt, answered. "My sister is too distraught. She told us to go ahead with her blessing."

To their surprise, there were no Roman soldiers guarding the opening of the tomb. The women looked at each other in alarm. Nothing was as it should be. Cautiously, they approached the opening of the tomb.

The women looked into the cave, holding out the lamps they'd brought. To their shock, two men were already inside. They were strangers. And they were sitting on the slab that should have contained Jesus' body. Startled, the women drew back.

"Don't be alarmed," one of the men said to them. "You are looking for Jesus the Nazarene, who was crucified. He has risen!" The ring of joy and triumph in his voice struck deep inside of Mary. Her heart leaped. "He is not here," the man continued. "See the place where they laid Him. But go, tell his disciples and Peter. He is going ahead of you into Galilee. There you will see Him just as He told you."

Frightened, the women collectively stumbled backward away from the men. Their motions were slow and measured at first. They were too afraid to speak. The reality of what the man said was too big to accept. Once out of the cave, they turned and fled down the hill. They were running from the shining men in the tomb as much as they were running to the disciples. The terror was overwhelming. Confusion swept over the group while they rushed as one down the hill.

"Who was that man? What does he mean that Jesus is risen?" Salome finally broke the silence.

"I don't know," Mary replied. "But we must go and tell the men." They ran as fast as they could to the place where the men were hiding and burst through the door.

"They have taken the Lord out of the tomb, and we don't know where they have put him!"

After a quick volley of questions that did nothing to clear the confusion, Peter and John rushed out of the room. The other disciples asked her friends for more details as she ran out behind the men. Peter and John were way ahead of her. Already tired and out of breath from the previous run, she followed more slowly.

Dawn was in the air. The sun would be up soon. Pushing to run faster, she looked and saw John ducking to see into the tomb. Peter caught up to him and entered the opening. John followed. After a few seconds, they both came back out. She climbed the hill, eager to look into the tomb. As she approached, the men wore bewildered expressions and murmured between themselves, speculating on what could have happened. They didn't even notice her as she passed by. Mary watched them leave, still talking between themselves. They sounded afraid.

Overwhelmed with sorrow to see Jesus' body was really missing, she began to weep. Would she not get the honor of anointing her Lord's body?

Wouldn't she have a chance to say a proper goodbye to her Lord? Everything had been so rushed on Friday as they hurried to keep the Sabbath, she never had that final moment of closure. Joseph and Nicodemus had taken care of Him, and she had done nothing. In her heart, she'd already been planning this moment to give him a proper burial. She desperately wanted to honor Jesus one last time for everything that He had done for her. She looked into the tomb again. The first rays of dawn lightened the heavy darkness outside, but she anticipated needing her lamp to look inside the tomb. Strangely, a glow seemed to fill the chamber when she peered in. She was alarmed to see the same two men inside.

"Woman, why are you crying?"

This time, too grief-stricken to run away in fear, she decided to ask them where she could find Jesus. Vaguely, she wondered if Peter and John had also talked to these men.

With a trembling voice, she answered, "They have taken my Lord away, and I don't know where they have put Him."

The men didn't answer. They simply smiled at her. Light was emanating from them, but she was too distracted to make much of it.

When it became obvious that these strange men would not speak to her again, Mary backed out of the tomb. Mary turned around and uncontrollable sobs overtook her. Through the veil of tears, she saw another man. The rising sun shone behind him, and she couldn't see his face. Too distraught with grief to be frightened or self-conscious, she tried to walk around him to go back down the hill.

"Woman, why are you crying? Who is it you are looking for?"

Maybe he was the gardener and he could help her. Maybe he was the one who had taken Jesus away. Hope stirred in her. Perhaps this man could lead her to the Lord. Sobbing unashamedly, she leaned against a huge rock and covered her face with her hands. She begged, "Sir, if you have carried him away, tell me where you have put Him, and I will get Him."

"Mary!"

That voice! She turned toward Him. Before her mind registered what was happening, her heart cried out, "Rabboni!" It was Him!

No one else said her name like He did. That voice... it was Jesus! She flung herself toward the glorious sound and stumbled because she couldn't see through her tears. As joy flooded through her, her knees gave away and she fell at His feet. Flinging her arms around His feet, she cried uncontrollably.

She couldn't believe this was real. How could He stand here, calling her name? Three days ago, she'd watched Him take His last breath. She'd watched as the soldiers pierced His side, and blood and water had gushed out, confirming that He was truly dead. Hadn't she cried out in despair to see the evidence of His death? She saw the men bring His limp body down from the cross, their robes bloodied in the process. She'd seen them bury Him in the tomb and roll a stone across the opening.

A hand rested on her head, a gentle caress. "Do not hold onto me, for I have not yet returned to the Father. Go instead to my brothers and tell them I am returning to my Father and your Father, to my God and your God."

Mary let go of His feet and struggled to her knees. He was gone. She cried out in alarm. Had it been a dream? Was her grief causing hallucinations? Slowly, she stood up. Maybe she was losing her mind. The shining men in the tomb, talking to a dead man, and the disappearing Jesus. Mary looked down at the ground where Jesus had been standing and saw His footprints. She shook her head. No, she hadn't been hallucinating. Jesus had been here talking to her. It was real. Jesus was alive!

"Mary!" She looked down the hill. Her friends were coming back.

"What's going on? Peter and John said the tomb was empty and they didn't see the shining men we saw." In a daze, Mary walked forward to join them.

The pinkish light of the early sun seemed to set the whole world aglow, adding to the strange sense of other-worldliness.

Her friends had caught up to her. "I saw Him," Mary said, "I swear, I saw Him and He talked to me."

After a brief moment of shock, all the women spoke at once. Questions came at her with such a rapid pace she couldn't answer any of them.

She kept repeating, "I saw Him. I heard Him. I even touched Him. He's alive. He has risen!" Her friends' faces turned from disbelief, shock to joyous acceptance as she adamantly proclaimed her experience.

"I believe you," Joanna finally said with conviction. "I believe you!" Then she laughed. "Mary, I believe you! That's the only thing that makes sense about this whole morning! He did tell us this would happen, didn't He? He did tell us!"

Mary laughed, too, and delirious mirth filled her. These last few days, particularly this morning, her heart had felt extreme grief, extreme shock, and now extreme joy. Their tears turned to contagious laughter until the whole group was hit with hilarity. They jumped up and down in ecstatic expression of relief and joy.

"I don't know what this means, but let's go! We have to tell the men!" The other Mary grabbed her hand and pulled her down the hill. The whole group of women rushed as one toward town. As they made their way downhill, laughter turned to silence as uncertainty settled on them. The awesomeness of the moment was quite sobering. A vague sense of disquiet filled them. Maybe they were losing their minds. If only they could see Jesus for themselves.

They reached the bottom of the hill.

"Greetings." A man stood before them.

This time, Mary knew it was Jesus. She recognized His voice. With a cry, she was the first one to fall at His feet. As soon as she fell to her face, she heard her friends also cry out and follow suit. Spontaneous worship broke out as they proclaimed Him to be God. They cried, they worshipped, they begged Him to stay. Jesus received their worship, allowing the overflow of emotions to settle. When the initial outburst of terror and joy had passed, gentle hands rested on each of their heads in turn.

In a soothing, reassuring voice, Jesus said, "Don't be afraid. Go and tell my brothers to go to Galilee; there they will see me."

Jesus disentangled Himself from their embrace and disappeared again. In silent awe, the women remained on their knees. For a long moment, they were still like statues as awestruck wonder flowed through them. Each of their hearts were filled with gratitude, and helpless yearning for the One who had just left. His footprints were still visible in the dirt where He had received their adoring worship.

God...it was real. Jesus was alive!

In the silence, Mary said, "It's true. He truly is the Son of God."

There's Something About Mary

Quite a bit of controversy surrounds Mary, the Mother, and Mary Magdalene, the Apostle; more than any other figures in the New Testament. Jesus' mother is obviously a source of division among the Catholics and the Protestants. But Mary Magdalene garners more than her share of controversy.

In the Early Church, Mary Magdalene was called "apostola apostolorum" which translates to "apostle of the apostles" or "apostle to the apostles." For several hundred years, it was a well-received fact that Mary Magdalene was one of the founding apostles of the Church.

There's also some debate about her surname "Magdalene." Does it refer to what could have been her hometown, Magdala, or does it refer to the Hebrew word "migdal" which means "tower, fortress, elevated, great?" There are many unanswered questions about this woman. She is often mistaken for the woman who'd lived a sinful life who attended Simon the Pharisee's dinner and anointed Jesus' feet with oil. There's even speculation that the adulteress saved from stoning in John 8 was Mary Magdalene.

What adds to the confusion is that there are numerous Marys in the gospels. There's Mary, the mother of Jesus, Mary, the wife of Clopas who is also Mary the mother's sister. There's Mary of Bethany, who is named as one who anointed Jesus with oil but not His feet. This Mary anointed Jesus' head. Then we have Mary Magdalene who is the only person identified in each of the four gospels as being present at Jesus' crucifixion.

Paul also mentioned a Mary in his greetings at the end of Romans. He commended Mary for being a hard worker. Most scholars believe that this was Mary Magdalene.

What's up with all the Marys? In Jesus' day, four out of every ten girls were named Mary. The root meaning of Mary stems from the Hebrew word "mara," which means "bitter." It often reflected the parents' disappointment in having a daughter instead of a desired son. In Mary, Jesus' mother's case, her father must have been extremely disappointed because he named at least two of his daughters by the same name.

It's not really surprising that in this cultural backdrop Jesus would have multiple Marys in His life. Pretty much everyone in Israel had multiple Marys in their lives. In a culture that prized conformity and uniformity above unique individuality, popular names tended to be used over and over again until you had several people in the same family sharing the same name.

It was also considered a great honor to name offspring after a relative. Hence, it was fairly common for families to carry the same names on through the generations. Case in point, the two Marys who were sisters both had sons named James; James the Greater and James the Lesser. They both played major roles in the Early Church. That's not to be confused with James, the son of Zebedee, who was Jesus' disciple.

Also, when John the Baptist was born, his father and mother had to fight their community that protested against the name "John." The villagers' logic was that no one in their family had the name "John" so how could Zechariah and Elizabeth want to name their son "John?"

Can you see why it's so hard to keep track of all the different people with the same names? Now, let's focus our attention on the specific Scriptural references to Mary Magdalene. What does the Holy Spirit record for us regarding this woman who had the privilege of being the first one to see Jesus resurrected?

Jesus Discipled Women

Luke 8:1-3 tells us that Mary was one of the women who "were helping to support them (Jesus and the disciples) out of their own means." She is listed in this group of financial supporters with Susana and Joanna, the wife of an official in Herod's court. We know that there were more than these three because Luke says, "and many others." Within the context of this passage, the "many others" Luke is referring to are women. Jesus had a group of women disciples who followed Him, supported Him, and were a part of His ministry. These women obviously were well-to-do. They supported thirteen men in their traveling ministry and also supported themselves.

It's an interesting fact to ponder. In Jesus' day, women were not really considered fully human. Their testimony was not acceptable in the court of law. Generally speaking, families didn't value their daughters enough to educate them. Rabbis taught their students to pray thanksgiving prayers for not being born a woman. A man could divorce a woman for displeasing him by simply declaring "I divorce you" three times and giving her a certificate of divorce. Women did not have the same rights to divorce their husbands. Yet, Jesus traveled with a retinue of women who were His disciples. He took His time and effort to disciple women when they weren't allowed to lead, teach, or join the men's section of the synagogues where the Torah was studied. It says something about Jesus to me.

These well-to-do women, who must have had comfortable homes of their own, were willing to travel the dusty roads and camp out in the most uncomfortable places just to be with Jesus. They left their husbands and families to be with Jesus. They risked ridicule and rejection from the crowds to be with Jesus. What this tells me is that these women liked to be with Jesus more than they disliked the circumstances surrounding Him. He was worth the risk and the sacrifice.

Something about the way He related to them made the inconvenience and social ridicule worthwhile. They must have felt a love from Him they didn't receive anywhere else. When we fall genuinely in love with someone who also makes us feel well-loved, everything can feel like a joyous adventure. I think Jesus made them feel like they were on a grand adventure with Him. And He genuinely enjoyed their company. He truly is the most compelling person to ever walk the earth.

In the same passage in Luke, we're told that Jesus cast seven demons out of Mary Magdalene. Some have speculated that the number seven represents the completion of evil, such as the seven deadly sins, so Mary must have been in very deep demonic bondage. This was a woman who had lived a life completely tormented by evil forces and had finally found freedom when Jesus entered her life. We don't really know what led to her deliverance and how she came to follow Him. What we do know is that this deliverance birthed in Mary such a profound gratitude that she became Jesus' disciple.

. . .

Just Another Disciple

In the accounts of Jesus' crucifixion, the four gospels give us different perspectives. Each author records unique aspects of the trial, the crucifixion, and the resurrection. Matthew and John were eyewitnesses to the events. Many scholars believe that the gospel of Mark may have been penned by Mark, but the voice behind the gospel was actually Peter's. So there's a chance that we have an account of Jesus' life and His Passion from three eyewitness accounts. If Luke had been a follower of Christ who didn't achieve prominence until after Jesus' resurrection, then the four gospels could all be eyewitness accounts.

It's a fascinating study and piece together a coherent timeline based on these different accounts. When we do, what is striking is that each one records Mary Magdalene as having a front-row seat to the Passion of Christ. She was there when they tried and sentenced Jesus. She was there, watching in the distance, when they nailed Him to the cross. She drew nearer still when He was lifted high for all to see. And she was there when Jesus took His final breath.

Mary watched as Joseph of Arimathea and Nicodemus, secret followers of Christ who strangely came out of hiding upon Jesus' death, took her Lord's body and laid Him in a tomb. She was there first thing Sunday morning to make certain that Jesus would receive a proper burial. When men ran away in fear, and family members stayed behind, Mary chose to be there.

Some are prone to believing Dan Brown's theory that Mary was loyal because she was Jesus' wife. This theory makes no sense. When Mary first saw the resurrected Jesus, she didn't respond as a wife. She didn't embrace Him and call Him intimate names as a wife would her husband. She fell at His feet and she worshiped Him. She called Him "Rabboni" or Teacher, like any other disciple would. The terms of their relationship are clear. He was the Teacher. She was the pupil. In short, she was His loyal disciple.

During Jesus' ministry, He healed many and cast out numerous demons. He fed thousands, taught the multitudes, and laid hands on countless children. But few exhibited gratitude like Mary Magdalene. When others received healing, they thanked Jesus, professed belief in Him, then went home to go back to their lives. Mary gave up everything she had and chose to be Jesus' disciple. She didn't just believe. She surrendered. She held nothing back. Everything she had belonged to Jesus.

I wonder if this is why, when Jesus awoke from death, He chose to reveal Himself to Mary first. So much debate surrounds the fact that Jesus told Mary to go and tell the disciples, His "brothers", that He had risen. Does this mean that she is the first commissioned apostle? Does this mean that Jesus was elevating women to the same level as men when a woman's testimony wasn't valid in that day and age? Does this mean women are supposed to preach the Gospel just as much as the men? I suppose it could mean all of that. As a woman, it's nice to reflect on those points and feel validated by Jesus Himself as a credible witness for the Gospel. But that's beside the point. It's peripheral to the real story that unfolded.

The Beloved One

Mary longed to be with Jesus when He was a popular Rabbi healing the sick and feeding the poor. She longed to be with Jesus when He was in the midst of persecution. Even when He died, she longed to be with Jesus to honor His broken body. She lived a life filled with gratitude, and she never wavered in her love. Roman soldiers, angry mobs, and religious leaders had no sway over her. She would worship her Lord Jesus and follow Him wherever He went.

Jesus commended the woman in Luke 8. He said, "Her many sins have been forgiven for she loved much." In this story, Jesus asked Simon a question. Who would love more? The one who's been forgiven little or the one who's been forgiven much? Simon answered correctly that the one who'd been forgiven much would love the Master more. This could be why Mary Magdalene is so often confused with this anonymous woman. Because Mary also showed that she loved much because she had been healed and forgiven of much.

Peter denied Jesus three times after boasting that no one else loved Jesus as much as he did. The other disciples stayed away from the trial, the sentencing, and even the resurrection. The only two consistent figures who stood by Jesus until the end are John, who identified himself as the disciple whom Jesus loved, and Mary Magdalene.

It was not the ones who boasted in their own love that ended up being faithful to the end. The ones who stayed and remained true to the end knew that they were the beloved of Jesus.

Mary wasn't there because she was boasting in her love for Jesus. Mary was there because no one else had ever loved her like Jesus had loved her.

Going Deeper

1. Do you remember when you first genuinely felt that Jesus loved you? How did His love become personal for you?

2. Have you ever been persecuted for your faith in Jesus? Has following Jesus cost you anything? Share your experience and share how Jesus showed up for you in the midst of the persecution.

3. Mary was delivered from many demons. What has Jesus delivered you from?

4. Have you been called into ministry or leadership by God when people may have resisted that call? Share your journey and how God is confirming His call on your life.

Prayer of Blessing

Father, thank you that you've never seen any of your children as lesser than others. Thank you for the resources you've supplied. We dream of living such an abundant life that we can resource your Kingdom on earth even as Mary Magdalene was a financial provider for Jesus' ministry. We ask that you would enrich our lives in every way so that we can be the providers for Kingdom ministry. We receive inventions, innovative ideas, and promotions that will set us up to be as Mary was. We desire to resource renewal, revival, and reformation. We desire to disciple our cities, nation, and the world with the good news of the gospel. We want to see people healed, delivered, and commissioned for the sake of the gospel. We want to be the solution to the world's issues because of the Holy Spirit who lives in us. We declare that, as your Word states, we are the head and not the tail, the lenders and not the borrowers. We declare that we are good stewards for Kingdom finances, gifts, and relationships. We position ourselves to receive increase and abundance and we covenant with you to be blessings on this earth. We agree with your will for increasing abundant life and gladly receive all Jesus' death and resurrection purchased for us.

References:

Luke 8:1-3

1 Soon afterwards, He *began* going around from one city and village to another, proclaiming and preaching the kingdom of God. The twelve were with Him, **2** and *also* some women who had been healed of evil spirits and sicknesses: Mary who was called Magdalene, from whom seven demons had gone out, **3** and Joanna the wife of Chuza, Herod's steward, and Susanna, and many others who were contributing to their support out of their private means.

Matthew 27:55-61

Burial of Jesus

55 Many women were there looking on from a distance, who had followed Jesus from Galilee while ministering to Him. **56** Among them was Mary Magdalene, and Mary the mother of James and Joseph, and the mother of the sons of Zebedee.

Jesus Is Buried

57 When it was evening, there came a rich man from Arimathea, named Joseph, who himself had also become a disciple of

Jesus. **58** This man went to Pilate and asked for the body of Jesus. Then Pilate ordered it to be given *to him*. **59** And Joseph took the body and wrapped it in a clean linen cloth, **60** and laid it in his own new tomb, which he had hewn out in the rock; and he rolled a large stone against the entrance of the tomb and went away. **61** And Mary Magdalene was there, and the other Mary, sitting opposite the grave.

Matthew 28:1-10

Jesus Has Risen

1 Now after the Sabbath, as it began to dawn toward the first *day* of the week, Mary Magdalene and the other Mary came to look at the grave. **2** And behold, a severe earthquake had occurred, for an angel of the Lord descended from heaven and came and rolled away the stone and sat upon it. **3** And his appearance was like lightning, and his clothing as white as snow. **4** The guards shook for fear of him and became like dead men. **5** The angel said to the women, "Do not be afraid; for I know that you are looking for Jesus who has been crucified. **6** He is not here, for He has risen, just as He said. Come, see the place where He was lying. **7** Go quickly and tell His disciples that He has risen from the dead; and behold, He is going ahead of you into Galilee, there you will see Him; behold, I have told you."

8 And they left the tomb quickly with fear and great joy and ran to report it to His disciples. **9** And behold, Jesus met them and greeted them. And they came up and took hold of His feet and worshiped Him. **10** Then Jesus said to them, "Do not be afraid; go and take word to My brethren to leave for Galilee, and there they will see Me."

Mark 15:40-47

Death and Burial of Jesus

40 There were also *some* women looking on from a distance, among whom *were* Mary Magdalene, and Mary the mother of James the Less and Joses, and Salome. **41** When He was in Galilee, they used to follow Him and minister to Him; and *there were* many other women who came up with Him to Jerusalem.

Jesus Is Buried

42 When evening had already come, because it was the preparation day, that is, the day before the Sabbath, 43 Joseph of Arimathea came, a prominent member of the Council, who himself was waiting for the kingdom of God; and he gathered up courage and went in before Pilate, and asked for the body of Jesus. 44 Pilate wondered if He was dead by this time, and summoning the centurion, he questioned him as to whether He was already dead. 45 And ascertaining this from the centurion, he granted the body to Joseph.46 Joseph bought a linen cloth, took Him down, wrapped Him in the linen cloth and laid Him in a tomb which had been hewn out in the rock; and he rolled a stone against the entrance of the tomb.47 Mary Magdalene and Mary the *mother* of Joses were looking on *to see* where He was laid.

Mark 16:1-11

Jesus Has Risen

When the Sabbath was over, Mary Magdalene, and Mary the *mother* of James, and Salome, bought spices, so that they might come and anoint Him. 2 Very early on the first day of the week, they came to the tomb when the sun had risen. 3 They were saying to one another, "Who will roll away the stone for us from the entrance of the tomb?" 4 Looking up, they saw that the stone had been rolled away, although it was extremely large. 5 Entering the tomb, they saw a young man sitting at the right, wearing a white robe; and they were amazed. 6 And he said to them, "Do not be amazed; you are looking for Jesus the Nazarene, who has been crucified. He has risen; He is not here; behold, *here is* the place where they laid Him. 7 But go, tell His disciples and Peter, 'He is going ahead of you to Galilee; there you will see Him, just as He told you.'" 8 They went out and fled from the tomb, for trembling and astonishment had gripped them; and they said nothing to anyone, for they were afraid.

9 Now after He had risen early on the first day of the week, He first appeared to Mary Magdalene, from whom He had cast out seven demons. 10 She went and reported to those who had been with Him, while they were mourning and weeping.11 When they heard that He was alive and had been seen by her, they refused to believe it.

Luke 23:44-56

Death and Burial of Jesus

44 It was now about the sixth hour, and darkness fell over the whole land until the ninth hour, **45** because the sun was obscured; and the veil of the temple was torn in two. **46** And Jesus, crying out with a loud voice, said, "Father, into Your hands I commit My spirit." Having said this, He breathed His last. **47** Now when the centurion saw what had happened, he *began* praising God, saying, "Certainly this man was innocent." **48** And all the crowds who came together for this spectacle, when they observed what had happened, *began* to return, beating their breasts. **49** And all His acquaintances and the women who accompanied Him from Galilee were standing at a distance, seeing these things.

Jesus Is Buried

50 And a man named Joseph, who was a member of the Council, a good and righteous man **51** (he had not consented to their plan and action), *a man* from Arimathea, a city of the Jews, who was waiting for the kingdom of God; **52** this man went to Pilate and asked for the body of Jesus. **53** And he took it down and wrapped it in a linen cloth, and laid Him in a tomb cut into the rock, where no one had ever lain. **54** It was the preparation day, and the Sabbath was about to begin. **55** Now the women who had come with Him out of Galilee followed, and saw the tomb and how His body was laid. **56** Then they returned and prepared spices and perfumes. And on the Sabbath they rested according to the commandment.

Luke 24:1-12

Jesus Has Risen

1 But on the first day of the week, at early dawn, they came to the tomb bringing the spices which they had prepared. **2** And they found the stone rolled away from the tomb, **3** but when they entered, they did not find the body of the Lord Jesus. **4** While they were perplexed about this, behold, two men suddenly stood near them in dazzling clothing; **5** and as *the women* were terrified and bowed their faces to the ground, *the men* said to them, "Why do you seek the living One among the dead? **6** He is not here, but He has risen. Remember how He spoke to you while He was still in Galilee, 7 saying that the Son of Man must be delivered into the hands of sinful men, and be crucified, and the third day rise again." **8** And they remembered His words, **9** and returned from the tomb and reported all these things to the eleven and to all the rest. **10** Now they were Mary Magdalene and Joanna and Mary the *mother* of James; also the other women with them were telling these things to the apostles. **11** But these words appeared to them as nonsense, and they would not believe them. **12** But Peter got up and ran to the tomb; stooping and looking in, he saw the linen wrappings only; and he went away to his home, marveling at what had happened.

John 19:25-27

25 Therefore the soldiers did these things. But standing by the cross of Jesus were His mother, and His mother's sister, Mary the *wife* of Clopas, and Mary Magdalene. **26** When Jesus then saw His mother, and the disciple whom He loved standing nearby, He said to His mother, "Woman, behold, your son!" **27** Then He said to the disciple, "Behold, your mother!" From that hour the disciple took her into his own *household*.

John 20:1-18

The Empty Tomb

Now on the first *day* of the week Mary Magdalene came early to the tomb, while it was still dark, and saw the stone *already* taken away from the tomb. **2** So she ran and came to Simon Peter and to the other disciple whom Jesus loved, and said to them, "They have taken away the Lord out of the tomb, and we do not know where they have laid Him." **3** So Peter and the other disciple went forth, and they were going to the tomb. **4** The two were running together; and the other disciple ran ahead faster than Peter and came to the tomb first; **5** and stooping and looking in, he saw the linen wrappings lying *there*; but he did not go in. **6** And so Simon Peter also came, following him, and entered the tomb; and he saw the linen wrappings lying *there*, 7 and the face-cloth which had been on His head, not lying with the linen wrappings, but rolled up in a place by itself. **8** So the other disciple who had first come to the tomb then also entered, and he saw and believed. **9** For as yet they did not understand the Scripture, that He must rise again from the dead. **10** So the disciples went away again to their own homes.

Jesus Appears to Mary Magdalene

11 But Mary was standing outside the tomb weeping; and so, as she wept, she stooped and looked into the tomb; **12** and she saw two angels in white sitting, one at the head and one at the feet, where the body of Jesus had been lying. **13** And they said to her, "Woman, why are you weeping?" She said to them, "Because they have taken away my Lord, and I do not know where they have laid Him." **14** When she had said this, she turned around and saw Jesus standing *there*, and did not know that it was Jesus. **15** Jesus said to her, "Woman, why are you weeping? Whom are you seeking?" Supposing Him to be the gardener, she said to Him, "Sir, if you have carried Him away, tell me where you have laid Him, and I will take Him away." **16** Jesus said to her, "Mary!" She turned and said to Him in Hebrew, "Rabboni!" (which means, Teacher). **17** Jesus said to her, "Stop clinging to Me, for I have not yet ascended to the Father; but go to My brethren and say to them, 'I ascend to My Father and your Father, and My God and your God.'" **18** Mary Magdalene came, announcing to the disciples, "I have seen the Lord," and *that* He had said these things to her.

THE FORGIVEN

*T*he humiliation burned in her until a deep, silent rage began
to build. Anger took over the terror and the profound
shame of the moment. She closed her eyes, willing her mind to shut
out the shouts of accusations. Instead, she focused on her internal
fury.

She stood in the midst of the crowd, inside the temple courts, with
nothing but a thin blanket covering her. If she hadn't had the presence
of mind to drag the blanket with her in her tightly clenched fists, they
probably would have dragged her naked down the public streets and
not have cared. Of course, they wouldn't have cared! The thought
fueled her bitter animosity to a raging fire. Grinding her teeth, she
willed the fury to burn hotter.

If she was going to die, she would not die begging. Fierce pride
and wrath were much more preferable than terror and cowardice. She
kept repeating to herself, "I will not beg. I will not cry. I will not kneel
before them. They'll have to kill me before I fall at their feet!" Eyes
tightly closed, her hands fisted in front of her to keep the blanket
closed, she tried very hard to shut out the sounds around her.

"Teacher, this woman was caught in the act of adultery! In the Law,
Moses commanded us to stone such women. Now, what do you say?"

Silence.

She'd caught a brief glimpse of this man the hypocritical religious leaders were addressing before she'd closed her eyes. She hadn't been particularly impressed. Surrounded by a band of young men, he'd also seemed awfully young to be called a rabbi.

All the way here, her captors had been gloating that they would finally get the best of him. They were going to use her to trap this young rabbi. She was the perfect bait they needed. Her life didn't matter at all. Trapping this man in a religious error seemed to be a desperate need for these hypocrites. For a brief moment, she felt sorry for the fellow. But only for a moment. She couldn't afford to feel sorry for anyone else. Any softening in her heart might cause her to break. Then she would play the coward. God, she could not do that. She didn't want to die acting like a coward.

She concentrated on keeping her composure as the silence lengthened. She wondered if they'd succeed in trapping this rabbi. She knew that if this rabbi commanded her to be stoned, he would have to answer to the Romans. But if he exonerated her, he would have to answer to the Jews. Poor guy...he was as trapped as she. Maybe, in the end, they would die together. The mysterious silence was unbearable.

Opening her eyes, she slowly took in the scene around her. No one was watching her. Their eyes were glued to this young rabbi who was writing in the dirt. Truly strange. The temple courts were made of stone. Nothing could be read. Yet, He continued to write with his fingers as if everyone could read his words.

"If any one of you is without sin, let him be the first to throw a stone at her."

His words, said with a quiet, calm, yet firm authority she'd never heard before, caused her to view him with surprised respect. Her overloaded mind couldn't quite process what he'd said. Quickly, her eyes darted around the crowd, expecting to see a pharisee hurl a stone at her. Instead, the crowd seemed paralyzed.

An elderly Pharisee she had once looked up to was staring at this young rabbi. The look on his face changed from sneering anger to quiet shame. Eventually, he lowered his eyes and dropped the rock in his hand, making a rattling noise against the stones of the temple courtyard.

The sound rang loudly in the suddenly hushed crowd. The Pharisee slowly turned and walked away. After a small pause, another rock hit the stony ground. Another Pharisee left the mob. Then another. Soon, the whole crowd collectively dropped their rocks, and the loud rattle echoed across the temple. No one spoke. The last Pharisee remaining, the youngest of the group, looked bewildered, but followed the elders' example. He scurried away.

She couldn't believe what she'd just seen. Could this be true? They were going to let her go? Her head swung back to this remarkable rabbi, now standing, as he observed the Pharisees walk away. When the last of her accusers were gone, he turned, completely facing her.

His penetrating gaze left her feeling completely exposed. Vulnerable. Not because she was standing with nothing but a thin blanket covering her but because it felt like he was seeing into the innermost parts of her soul.

This young rabbi carried an extraordinary presence she had never encountered before. Yet this vulnerability he exposed didn't leave her feeling ashamed. Only known and completely understood. A feeling of utter warmth and acceptance swept over her. The rage she'd tried to hold onto melted, and she felt tears stinging her eyes. Her breath caught in her throat, and a small sob escaped her.

The kindness that emanated from him was too much for her when she'd expected judgment and contempt. Her emotions veered crazily. Now she feared having an emotional breakdown in front of complete strangers. She stood rigid with tension. Bracing against the explosion of emotions within her, she tried to hold onto her anger. Maybe this rabbi was setting her up. Maybe he was going to use her as other men had used her.

Defiantly, she glared at the man while she valiantly tried to still her trembling lips and stop the flow of tears. The silence lengthened as the young rabbi continued to look deeply into her eyes. She didn't like this feeling. Being physically naked didn't leave her feeling nearly as vulnerable as this sense of being emotionally exposed. She felt like he knew everything she'd ever done.

She broke his penetrating gaze and looked around her. His young disciples were frozen, too. They stood around their leader and were watching him with expectancy. They were not looking at her as she'd expected. Her eyes shifted back to the young rabbi.

Once their eyes met again, he walked towards her. She shrank back in fear. Was he going to strike her?

"Woman," he stood in front of her now. "Where are they? Is anyone condemning you?" The gentleness of his question, the tender reassurance in his voice, broke her. In spite of her resolve, her shoulders began to shake as her pent-up emotions erupted in the face of such unexpected tenderness. His expression was full of concern.

She was undone. Shaking her head in wonder, she sobbed, "No one, sir." She bowed her head in humility and surrender. He was being so kind.

She couldn't remember the last time a man had been kind to her. She couldn't stop crying. The violent sound of her own sobs filled the air. She clutched the thin blanket in front of her like a lifeline and wept away years of pain.

A gentle hand rested on her bowed head. It felt like the hand of blessing.

"Then neither do I condemn you. Go now and leave your life of sin."

She looked at him again. His intense gaze was full of love. She was sure he knew exactly what kind of woman she was. Yet, she felt complete acceptance from him. Her defenses crumbled. As she studied at her rescuer, a profound sense of gratitude overwhelmed her. His steady gaze never wavered as he poured healing compassion into the broken places of her soul.

Standing face to face with him, understanding dawned. This young rabbi, who'd faced an angry mob and successfully defended her, was giving her something that a woman in her position never received. Beyond rescuing her from harm and certain death, he was giving her a second chance.

. . .

The Defiant Adulteress

There's nothing like being caught in the midst of flagrant sin to make you feel the sting of shame. No glib excuse and no well-crafted justification can explain away the sin. You're just flat out caught. Whether we were young children or an adult caught in the middle of a white lie, most of us have experienced something like this. It's not hard to imagine what this woman must have felt when she was caught in the midst of adultery.

Imagine the horror of her shame being flaunted in public. Not only was she caught, but she was also dragged into the temple—the temple, for heaven's sake—for public judgment. That would be akin to being dragged into the Sunday morning church service wearing nothing but a sheet as your accusers expose your shame. What a traumatic experience!

When I read her story, I'm always struck by the fact that she's standing. And she remained standing throughout the whole story. Unlike that dramatic scene in the "Passion of the Christ" where the woman caught in adultery was face down on the ground, dragging herself across the dust to touch Jesus' feet, the Bible tells us that this woman remained standing. I see a certain defiance in that statement. She was caught, barely covered, and made the focus of an angry mob whose intention was to kill her. Not just because she sinned, but because they were using her to make a religious point. And she stood. Doesn't that strike you? It says something to me about her.

This woman didn't beg for her life. She didn't offer any justifications or explanations. She didn't cry out, "This isn't fair! What about the man? Why am I the only one being punished?" After all, adultery is a sin that requires a partner. She wasn't curled into a ball, and she wasn't weeping with fear. This woman faced the angry, murderous mob standing.

It's not just defiance I read. There's a sense of dignity about this woman. Though I'm not endorsing her sin, I admire the way she handled herself in the midst of a horrible situation. Few would've had the moxie to stand alone against a violent crowd. Something innate in us wants to cover up in a life-threatening situation. We want to hide. If we can't run and hide, we usually try to make ourselves as small as possible to feign a sense of security. But this woman resisted such impulses and faced her accusers with a defiant dignity.

I don't know if her attitude had any redeeming value. I'm not saying that being defiant about our sin is heroic. What I'm saying is that I think this woman had a lot of inner strength. Apparently, this inner strength was used to pursue forbidden activities with blatant disregard for God in order to satisfy her desires or meet her financial needs. But this strength also kept her from making a fool of herself in a horrifying situation. She faced her accusers with silence, refusing to be cowed. I like that about her.

There was a woman in Luke 7 who anointed Jesus' feet with oil. She wasn't named. Many have speculated that this unnamed woman was Mary Magdalene. Mel Gibson's "The Passion of the Christ" depicts Mary Magdalene as the adulteress saved from stoning. For the most part, theologians have debunked the theory that the woman who was rescued and the woman who anointed Jesus' feet was Mary Magdalene. Mary was such a well-known figure among Jesus' disciples; if she'd been involved in a story, the disciples would most likely have named her.

Though it wasn't Mary, I believe the woman who anointed Jesus' feet in Luke 7 and the adulteress who was rescued from the angry mob in John 8 was the same woman. Luke says that this woman had lived a sinful life. This woman was showing her gratitude by weeping at Jesus' feet and anointing Him with oil. Mary Magdalene showed her gratitude by financing Jesus and His disciples.

A Transformed Woman

When the adulteress left Jesus in John 8, she left with a commission. "Leave your life of sin," Jesus told her. Wouldn't it make sense that a woman who'd been rescued as she'd been would want to return and prove herself to Jesus? She left knowing that she'd received a second chance.

Her sin had been exposed in the most public way possible. Though her lover was spared a public trial, no doubt, wagging tongues would have exposed his identity to the community at large. She no longer had the option to go back to her former life even if she wanted to. Even with this public exposure of an illicit relationship, I don't think she left her life of sin because she had no choice. I think her encounter with Jesus radically transformed her. That reservoir of inner strength we see during her public trial would have been used to implement on the outside what had changed on the inside.

When she encountered the grace of Jesus Christ, her sin was framed in a completely different context than the religion of her day. Rather than the guilt, shame, and anger that accusation and condemnation breed, she would have been overwhelmed with gratitude. Guilt and shame never lead to genuine changes for the better. Only true forgiveness can transform.

Forgiveness from God and forgiveness of self releases us from cyclical bondages of sin. When Jesus challenged the self-righteous mob with the statement, "If any one of you is without sin, let him be the first to throw a stone at her," He reached into the deepest parts of the human conscience that went beyond the letter of the Law.

Those who burned with religious zeal suddenly came face to face with their own imperfections. They could not claim the status of being "without sin." Jesus had just placed every sin on the same level and obliterated any religious idea that the sin of behavior and the sin of intent had varying degrees of evil. In effect, they no longer had any moral high ground to stand on because they could not lay claim to a sinless life. This placed the adulteress and the accusers as equal in God's eyes. More importantly, in this situation, it placed them as equal in each other's eyes. Equal sinners.

Once Jesus accomplished this, the accusers didn't have a choice. They had to drop their stones and walk away. Their walking away also removed any grounds for future accusations. She was now free to face her accusers without shame. To shame her now would have been even more disgraceful for them. If they ever wagged their fingers at her or uttered accusations against her, she could simply challenge them in a way they would have no answer for: "Where was your stone?"

They voluntarily dropped the weapons of accusations and silently admitted their own sinfulness. Thus, her accusers were effectively silenced forever. This is the brilliance of what Jesus did. He didn't just rescue her from the moment. He completely delivered her and set her free to face a future without any fear of condemnation. Never would she have to fear reprisals for this public exposure of sin.

Her motive for changing her life would be gratitude. Truly, this is the only kind of change that actually lasts the test of time. We have no idea the price she paid for her sin. No doubt, her life was rocked and everything was turned upside down. Though her accusers could no longer stone her, certainly, her reputation would have been in tatters. She might as well have worn a scarlet letter. It would make perfect sense that she would be labeled "a woman who had lived a sinful life." Though God had forgiven her, I would venture to guess that the religious people of her day had not.

Their Law had been rendered powerless by Jesus, but I doubt their opinion of her had changed. It would be so easy to write another long interpretation of the scene at the Pharisee's house.

A Surrendered Life

There was celebration in the air. The house was full of people getting ready to dine on food and wine. People took their places at the dining table laden with dishes that fill the house with a delicious aroma. Men were inclining by the table, resting on their elbows. Women were bustling around the table serving bread and platters of food while servants were busily pouring wine.

Unobtrusively, a woman entered behind Jesus. She headed straight for His feet, and she broke the alabaster jar open. The aroma of food is slowly replaced with the pungent fragrance of the expensive perfume. She was rubbing Jesus' feet with the fragrance while sobbing with overwhelming emotions.

Everyone in the room looked around in curiosity and located the source of the scent. They saw a woman quietly weeping at Jesus' feet as she wiped them with her hair. The fragrant perfume overtook the house, and guests soon realized what she'd done. Oblivious to the attention and the murmurs of complaint and criticism, she continued to weep. She continued to wipe away the perfume and the tears from His feet with her hair. Her tears mingled with the oily perfume while her lips touched His feet with reverence. She was worshiping Jesus.

Defiantly, she'd stood while in a state of undress as the murderous intent of the crowd swelled around her. This same woman had her face at Jesus' feet in humble adoration and worship. Simon the Pharisee didn't wash Jesus' feet, a form of social insult towards a guest. But she rectified that. She gave Him the highest honor. His feet were too good for mere washing with water reserved for the common man. She bathed them with the most expensive perfume. She bathed them with sacrificial tears of love.

Scorning towels and cloth, she wiped His dirty feet with her own hair. In her absolute surrender and adoration of Jesus, the very fragrance she poured out on Jesus now clung to her. Her face bore the traces of tears poured out in gratitude. Her hands that broke the perfume jar into fragments and rubbed Jesus' feet, now smelled like the same perfume.

The dust that clung to Jesus' feet would now cling to hair strands that were used to towel them. All that marked Jesus now marked her. Here was a woman who refused to bow before an angry crowd. This woman no longer had any fear of man. Uncaring of the crowd, her only focus was to proclaim Jesus worthy of complete surrender and worship. No one else's opinion mattered. She loved Him. She wanted Him to know how much she loved Him. And Jesus understood it.

"She loved much," He said of her. Is there a greater reward than to hear Jesus say that He knows that we really love Him? The finger of

God that wrote the ten commandments on stone tablets wrote a message of grace on the stones of the temple courtyard.

We don't know exactly what He wrote. But the results speak for themselves. The Law that demanded death did not get its satisfaction on that day when Jesus wrote on stones once again. Jesus kept the Law at bay for another day when He Himself would pay the price for her sin on the cross at Calvary. He instituted the power of grace before its proper time when He delivered her from her accusers.

Her worship of Jesus revealed the heart of one who had truly experienced the power of grace. He offered her the one thing she needed the most. She didn't need anyone else's forgiveness. She needed His. She didn't need anyone else's approval. She needed to surrender to Him regardless of what others thought. She didn't need fine luxuries or even the necessities of life. She needed Jesus to know He was worthy of her all. After leaving her life of sin, by the blessing of Jesus, she needed more than an absence of accusation. She needed absolution. Jesus offered it to her freely as He does for us all.

He said, "Your sins are forgiven. Go in peace."

Going Deeper

1. Have you experienced public shame through the exposure of sin? If not you, has anyone close to you?

2. Is there something from your past others refuse to forget that keeps haunting you? How long ago was the act? Prayerfully ask the Lord how to handle condemnation of man when you know God has forgiven you. Are there steps you need to take to reconcile the wrongs committed?

3. Do you feel that God has truly forgiven you? If not, deal with this issue now and ask the Holy Spirit to cleanse your conscience as you meditate on what the cross means.

4. Is there any sexual sin for which you need forgiveness and resolution? If the sin is still present in your life, find someone who can counsel you and get the help you need. Remember that God is for you,

not against you. He desires your freedom and He's not angry with you.

5. Have you ever worshiped Jesus so extravagantly that others were offended or uncomfortable? Share what that felt like.

Prayer of Blessing

Father, thank you for forgiving us of our sins. Thank you that there is no condemnation in you, no shadow of turning away, and no fear of punishment. Thank you that Jesus dealt with our sins at the cross and we now walk in grace. We repent of all sexual sin and any other hidden sins. We receive the freedom you have for us. We ask for the restoration of our reputation and the genuine reconciliation of relationships that matter to us. We declare that you are the One we worship, you are the One we surrender to, and you are the One that does the miracle of transformation. We release your power of transformation and healing in every area of our lives. We declare that we are free of any fear of man and will worship you with wild abandon. Let our passions come fully alive in your presence that we may know the reason for being alive. Let our worship establish your Kingdom on earth as it is in heaven. We declare you to be worthy of such praise. All of creation is put on notice that Jesus Christ is the Lord of Lords and the King of Kings.

References:

John 8: 1-10

The Adulterous Woman

But Jesus went to the Mount of Olives. 2 Early in the morning He came again into the temple, and all the people were coming to Him; and He sat down and *began* to teach them. 3 The scribes and the Pharisees brought a woman caught in adultery, and having set her in the center *of the court*, 4 they said to Him, "Teacher, this woman has been caught in adultery, in the very act. 5 Now in the Law Moses commanded us to stone such women; what then do You say?" 6 They were saying this, testing Him, so that they might have grounds for accusing Him. But Jesus stooped down and with His finger wrote on the ground. 7 But when they persisted in asking Him, He straightened up, and said to them, "He who is without sin among you, let him *be the* first to throw a stone at her." 8 Again He stooped down and wrote on the ground. 9 When they heard it, they *began* to go out one by one, beginning with the older ones, and He was left alone, and the woman, where she was, in the center *of the court.* 10 Straightening up, Jesus said to her, "Woman, where are they? Did no one condemn you?"

Luke 7:36-50

Jesus Anointed by a Sinful Woman

36 Now one of the Pharisees was requesting Him to dine with him, and He entered the Pharisee's house and reclined *at the table.* 37 And there was a woman in the city who was a sinner; and when she learned that He was reclining *at the table* in the Pharisee's house, she brought an alabaster vial of perfume, 38 and standing behind *Him* at His feet, weeping, she began to wet His feet with her tears, and kept wiping them with the hair of her head, and kissing His feet and anointing them with the perfume. 39 Now when the Pharisee who had invited Him saw this, he said to himself, "If this man were a prophet He would know who and what sort of person this woman is who is touching Him, that she is a sinner."

Parable of Two Debtors

40 And Jesus answered him, "Simon, I have something to say to you." And he replied, "Say it, Teacher." 41 "A moneylender had two debtors: one owed five hundred denarii, and the other fifty. 42 When they were unable to repay, he graciously forgave them both. So which of them will love him more?" 43 Simon answered and said, "I suppose the one whom he forgave more." And He said to him, "You have judged correctly." 44 Turning toward the woman, He said to Simon, "Do you see this woman? I entered your house; you gave Me no water for My feet, but she has wet My feet with her tears and wiped them with her hair. 45 You gave Me no kiss; but she, since the time I came in, has not ceased to kiss My feet. 46 You did not anoint My head with oil, but she anointed My feet with perfume. 47 For this reason I say to you, her

sins, which are many, have been forgiven, for she loved much; but he who is forgiven little, loves little." **48** Then He said to her, "Your sins have been forgiven." **49** Those who were reclining *at the table* with Him began to say to themselves, "Who is this *man* who even forgives sins?" **50** And He said to the woman, "Your faith has saved you; go in peace."

THE RESURRECTED

*S*he should be the one in the coffin. It should have been her. *Life is useless,* she thought. Why had she been born? Her entire life had been filled with grief and sorrow. Everyone she loved was taken. Now, here lay her son. Her only son. God must truly hate her. Maybe, if He was truly merciful, He would take her next. Maybe even at the burial site she would keel over and die. Then she could join her family in Sheol and no longer live with the stigma of being a widow.

The thought brought such a thrill of hope in her that she cried out, "Lord, have mercy. Take me. Take me, too!"

The act of opening her mouth and crying out to God broke the silent, anguished dam of sorrow until she was wailing. Her knees hit the ground, and she grabbed her midsection as her body convulsed with uncontrollable grief.

The procession of mourners stopped to honor the mother grieving her only son. Her legs could no longer carry the burden of sorrow in her heart. She heard other people in the crowd weeping with her. It barely registered. The despair of her soul impregnated the atmosphere around her with oppressive heartbreak.

"Don't cry," a voice said. It cut across the cacophony of tribulation and penetrated her soul. She looked up, tears still streaming down her face, her mouth quivering with sobs. Through the waterfall of tears, she saw a man. He was watching her with such deep compassion, such a wealth of feeling, that it sent her into a fresh wave of sobs. Covering her face with her hands, she shook her head and doubled over again.

"Young man," the man said with commanding authority, "I say to you, get up!"

The air seemed to vibrate in response to this man's authority. Who was he talking to? In spite of herself, her head lifted. The man was standing next to her son, and he had his hands on the cloth covering the body.

The entire funeral procession stilled. Dubious yet intrigued, all eyes were on the stretcher. In the stillness, the cloth moved. Those carrying the body reacted in fright and practically dropped the stretcher to the ground.

Another movement from the basket. Gasps of shock reverberated through the crowd. Her heart leapt. Was her son coming back to life? He'd been dead since early evening the day before. Throughout the night, she'd sat in vigil next to his cold body, unable to accept that he was gone. Just this morning, her friends and family had come to pry her away and wrapped his precious body in grave clothes. Yet, her son was stirring as if life was returning to his body, as if God had taken pity on her and had finally heard her desperate prayers.

Without even standing to her feet, she crawled and scrambled across the dirt to get closer to the open coffin. Her son sat up. "I can't see. Get this off of me."

It was her son's voice! With frantic hands, her breath coming in gasps, she took the cloth off of him.

Her son looked back at her. His eyes were blinking as he adjusted to the sunlight. He was alive! He was breathing and moving! Her son looked around the crowd and asked, "Mom, what's going on?"

Throwing her arms around him, babbling with joy, she wept again. This time, she was crying with tears of joy. Her entire being leapt from despair to life. She couldn't stop hugging her son, stroking him to make sure he was alive. She grabbed his face in her hands and looked into his deep brown eyes with wonder and awe.

"You're alive!" Kissing his face, embracing him, she reveled in the sudden change of fortune. A miracle beyond her wildest dream had just happened!

Once the shock of the resurrection settled, and it truly became real that her son was alive, she looked for the man with the voice. Though others were praising God and calling him a prophet, the man kept his eyes fastened on her.

He looked like peace in the midst of a storm. Tears ran down his face, too, and he was smiling at her. His face radiated joy. As her eyes looked into His with stupefied wonder, all she could think in her heart was, "You must be God."

A Widow's Plight

Sometimes, questions about the stories in the Bible remain just that. Questions. God doesn't make a habit of answering our questions. When I read the story of the widow from Nain, I want to know how old the widow was. How long had she been a widow?

Had her husband passed away recently? Maybe even from the same disease that struck her only son? Or had she been a single mom who raised her son as faithfully as she could with meager resources? Did she have daughters? In a culture that valued sons as resources and saw daughters as liabilities, had she put her hopes on her only son? My imagination runs wild as I think about this story.

We don't know much about her. But the things we know paint a bleak picture. Nain was a small town not known for its wealth. More than likely, she was very poor. She was also a widow. This woman who had lost her husband was now living through the shock of losing her only son. Apparently, she was pretty well liked because the Bible tells us that "a large crowd from the town was with her."

It's not so much the specifics about this woman that tugs at the heart. It's the circumstances surrounding her that rings a universal bell. What mother can't understand the grief of losing a child. Even if we have never lived through such tragedy, who would not understand that this is perhaps the greatest tragedy of humanity? The double tragedy is that she is a widow. She was abandoned by two men she loved the most to the finality of death. With a story like this, we don't need a whole lot of details to have our hearts immediately drawn into the drama.

During the time of Jesus, people were not buried in a closed lid coffin. Most often, they would wrap their dead in a cloth and place them in a basket. The basket was carried on a stretcher to a cave and buried with a stone rolled across the opening; much like the tomb Jesus was laid in upon His death. When Jesus walked into this funeral procession, the stretcher was holding an uncovered basket with the body of the young man covered in cloth.

When the Bible says, "He went up and touched the coffin," more than likely He laid hands on the young man's body. I don't know why this moves me so. As He had proven with Lazarus, He could have simply called out for the dead to awaken and life would have returned to the body. Yet Jesus chose to lay hands on this boy. Jesus often does that. He chooses to touch when touching was forbidden and would have made him a social pariah.

Ceremonial law would have dictated that Jesus go through a cleansing ritual for a period of time when He touched a dead body. The conundrum presented in this situation is that this dead body came alive! How would they apply their religious laws when there was a resurrection? When Jews touched anything unclean, such as those suffering from disease, the law mandated a period of cleansing that also required isolation from society. With Jesus, this law rarely applied. When Jesus touched the unclean, they became clean. When He laid hands on the sick, they became well. And when He touched the dead, they were raised to life. Jesus absolutely defied every religious expectation with supernatural solutions.

Human Grief Attracts Divine Compassion

A unique aspect of this story is that this widow did not go seeking

Jesus. Jesus sought her. While the other two resurrections recorded in the New Testament tell the story of people who went looking for Jesus, this story is of a woman who may have never heard of Him. She never asked for His help. Likewise, Jesus didn't ask for permission to raise her son from the dead. No person's faith for a miracle was involved in this resurrection.

Jesus saw her circumstances and deeply empathized with her grief, and He did what only He could do. This isn't a story about faith. It's a story about Jesus' willingness, compassion, and power in the midst of profound brokenness in creation that should never have experienced death.

The gospels only record four miracles Jesus performed where He took the initiative. The first of these is the story of this widow from Nain. Luke also records in Chapter Twelve an encounter on a Sabbath Day with a woman who had been crippled for eighteen years. Jesus called out to her across the temple courts, "Woman, you are set free from your infirmity!" John gives us the other two accounts; the paralytic by the pool of Bethesda, and the man who had been born blind. However, none of these other stories record Jesus' emotional state. Only in the story of the widow of Nain do we get that, "His heart went out to her."

There's something almost impulsive about this story that captures my attention. It's as if Jesus had no idea what He would encounter on that day. He saw the widow's plight, He heard her loud wailings of heart-crushing grief, and He was so moved, He entreated her, "Don't cry."

While others could only offer noises of sympathy, Jesus could deliver. He not only said, "Don't cry," He removed the reason for her tears. He literally turned her tears of sorrow into tears of joy. He brought life back to the lifeless.

Religion Robs Human Compassion

The religious traditions of her culture taught that those who suffered were being punished for their sins by God. To lose a husband

and be left a widow was viewed as a curse. Now to lose her son, her only son, how the villagers must have viewed her with suspicion! The judgment and condemnation would have increased over time. She would not only deal with unimaginable grief, she would have faced religious and social persecution, and become an outcast.

Did this widow feel like she was God's number one enemy? Could she ever believe that God loved her? A million scenarios must have run through her mind as she wondered what she had done that was so terrible that God would punish her so. Guilt and shame, grief, and sorrow were a few of her most intimate friends. Who could free her from the accusations, the oppressive weight of condemnation? The thoughtless and cruel words of "comfort" about God's justice and His ways would have been nothing compared to the self-loathing that would have filled her.

The disciples asked Jesus, "Who sinned, this man or his parents?"

Jesus answered, "Neither this man nor his parents sinned but this happened that the work of God may be displayed in his life." (John 9:2-3)

Jesus rebuked the predominant teaching that all suffering was caused by someone's sin. He taught that sometimes suffering is allowed to happen so that God's work may be displayed. A fallen world has strange illnesses and circumstances contrary to the original intent of God. The mystery of suffering would never be fully answered this side of heaven. God did not originate suffering and He did not punish with suffering. They even had the book of Job to teach them that. Yet, the human arrogance of ego remained entrenched among the Jews. Who sinned? Whose fault is this? What did I do to cause this? What can I do to fix it? The hand of God was often seen as a hand of punishment. And self was viewed as the cause and the solution. Then Jesus came.

The Father's Heart and the Grieving Mother

Jesus came to reveal the heart of the Father who seeks to find, forgive, heal, and love. Jesus displayed God's goodness in the midst of horrific pain and sorrow. He displayed a Father willing to raise the dead to life when no one had the faith to ask. He displayed the heart of the Father who weeps with those who weep and rejoices with those who rejoice. Jesus showed that God hates suffering more than we do and that He would do anything to take the suffering away from us. That's why Jesus came. To show the love of the Father.

I wonder how this widow's life changed after her son was resurrected. I imagine that she became one of Jesus' followers. Who knows? Maybe she was one of the women who stood on a hill and watched as Jesus was crucified. Maybe, through her tears of grief, she had once again prepared spices and oil for the burial of another man that she'd loved and lost. And maybe, just maybe, she'd been a part of the group of women to whom Jesus had revealed His glorified self. Paul records that there were five hundred witnesses to Jesus' resurrection (1 Corinthians 15:6.) I wonder if she'd been one of them. I suppose if it was my son who had died and Jesus had brought him back to life, I would have become one of His most ardent followers.

The widow of Nain compels me because she reminds me of those moments in my life when grief struck so forcefully, when heartbreak was so complete, I thought my own soul had died. In those moments, when I had no awareness of the Lord, only the specter of death crushing me, Jesus entered.

Something about this kind of devastating grief becomes a welcome mat for our Jesus. He doesn't wait for an open invitation. He is drawn to our tears. The shattered heart that knows no life is an invitation for His resurrection life to enter. He doesn't only say in the most tender whisper, "Daughter, don't cry," He also sheds tears and weeps with us. He not only weeps with us, He alone who can, does the impossible and brings joy out of sorrow. He surprises us with a miracle when we are least expecting it.

Jesus doesn't need to be begged. He's already willing. Jesus doesn't wait for us to get it together. He offers the way out. Jesus doesn't wait for an invitation. He's already here.

The widow of Nain could have been just another woman who lost loved ones that society would forget. History had no reason to record her, and her story was not unique in this sin devastated world to be worth noting. But because of Jesus, her story is not recorded in human history, but in the eternal Word of God. Her story has become the beacon of hope for us who have experienced the sting of death. The Father's heart for a grieving mother resulted in resurrection. It is this God who has absolutely conquered death who draws us to Himself.

Going Deeper

1. Have you ever lost a loved one to death? How did Jesus meet you in that place?

2. Have you experienced God's intervention in your life when you weren't asking or praying?

3. Do you have superstitions about the wrath of God you need to let go? For instance, when things go wrong, do you entertain the idea that God is punishing you for your sins? What does the Bible say?

4. Are there dreams that have died that are actually God-dreams for you that need the resurrection power of Jesus? Identify the dreams that need to come back to life and pray for blessings and favor.

Prayer of Blessing

Father, thank you that death and hell have been completely defeated and you rule over all realms. Thank you that we do not have to fear eternal separation because you reconciled us to yourself. We stand on the finished work of the cross and bless you that we are now children of grace. We receive the life you have for us. We invite your resurrection power to raise to life areas in our lives that are dead. We ask that you would breathe hope and life into God-given destinies and purposes. We agree with your will and your plans for our lives and repent of letting go and quitting. We rebuke the voice of death and refuse to partner with the enemy that seeks to kill, steal and destroy. We declare resurrection over dead dreams, relationships, and ideas. We declare that we are highly favored, chosen, and blessed and you're attracted to our places of need. As we delight in you, we anticipate that the desires of our hearts will be fulfilled. We bless your name, Jesus, and abide in your unfailing love.

References:

Luke 7:11-17

Jesus Raises a Widow's Son

11 Soon afterwards He went to a city called Nain; and His disciples were going along with Him, accompanied by a large crowd. 12 Now as He approached the gate of the city, a dead man was being carried out, the only son of his mother, and she was a widow; and a sizeable crowd from the city was with her. 13 When the Lord saw her, He felt compassion for her, and said to her, "Do not weep." 14 And He came up and touched the coffin; and the bearers came to a halt. And He said, "Young man, I say to you, arise!" 15 The dead man sat up and began to speak. And *Jesus* gave him back to his mother. 16 Fear gripped them all, and they *began* glorifying God, saying, "A great prophet has arisen among us!" and, "God has visited His people!" 17 This report concerning Him went out all over Judea and in all the surrounding district.

CONCLUSION

*T*hank you for taking the time to read my book. My hope is that it has offered you a fresh perspective and insight into the role of women in the Bible. My prayer is that coming generations will treat all humanity with equal regard and release the unique gifting and talents in each person regardless of gender, race, or social status. I yearn to see the Body of Christ exemplify genuine freedom in living the life God intended for us. I don't want God's Word to be used to continuously oppress, control, and diminish those that are precious to Him. I believe learning to value mothers, daughters, and sisters as equal members in God's family is an important priority in establishing a genuine Kingdom. A deeper study of the Hebrew words in the Creation story brought this point home for me.

The first chapter of Genesis says: *God created man in His own image, in the image of God He created him; male and female He created them.* (Genesis 1:27 NASB)

Even at first glance, this verse clearly states that both male and female were created in the image of God. Christians constantly repeat this verse and agree that all of humankind bears the image of God. Yet, if anyone refers to the God-head in the feminine pronoun, that person is accused of being a heretic, a new age believer who worships the feminine, or a false teacher who needs to be avoided at all costs.

For some reason, all of the English translations of the Bible refer to the three persons of the God-head in the masculine. Of course, we know that the original language of the Bible is Hebrew, not English. Though every English translation offers profound insights into the Word of God, translations can carry biases that have washed out the original meaning of the written Word of God. One of the most glaring changes is the translation of the word "ruach." In the original language, "ruach" is a feminine noun much as the word "woman" is understood in English as a feminine noun. Yet, for whatever reason, English translators continue to refer to "ruach" in the masculine.

Perhaps the hang-up stems from the fact that "ruach" is most often understood in Christendom as the "Holy Spirit." In fact, after the word "Elohim" is introduced in Genesis 1:1, which introduces that God is more than one person, "ruach" is the first Person of the Trinity introduced in the Creation story (Genesis 1:2). The word "ruach" is used more than 370 times in the Hebrew language. The Hebrew language assigns masculine or feminine attributes to their words. Romantic languages based on Latin, like French, Italian, and Spanish, also identify masculine and feminine aspects in their languages. In Hebrew, the word "ruach" is clearly a feminine noun.

I find this translation bias to be of disservice to our fundamental understanding of the nature of God. If male and female are both created truly in the image of God, where is the source of femininity? Why is it so blasphemous to refer to the Holy Spirit as a "she" and not a "he" when the original language reveals this to be true? Whenever this subject is discussed, unfailingly, I am accused of being a heretic. Yet, my quest is to be as true to the original revelation of God as possible. Western Christianity does not define God. Only God defines God. And there is a distinct Person in the Trinity, revealed as a feminine Spirit. In this hour, we must continue to dig deep into the word of God and not be afraid to root out deeply entrenched biases that are direct lies perpetuated by the enemy to cripple the body of Christ.

· · ·

It's Time for Change

Throughout human history, women have been treated as second class citizens. Many religious systems relegate women as the lesser of the human species. Sadly, even Christianity, based on the new covenant of grace that was purchased by the blood of our precious Savior Jesus Christ often defaults to a theology that embraces misogyny. I say this is a sad reality because Jesus specifically came to break all curses. The Bible is clear that the outpouring of the Holy Spirit at Pentecost was intended to equalize men, women, and children as members of the same Kingdom and crucial parts of the same family of God.

The earliest church history records many stories of women who were released into leadership. Women were apostles (Junias in Romans 16), women were church planters (Lydia in Acts 16), women were prophets (Philip's four daughters in Acts 21), and teachers of the Word (Priscilla in Acts 18). Such leadership positions for women were unprecedented in the Judaic religion and the Hebrew culture. Yet, the early church recognized that Jesus had come to set all of humanity free. Everyone with spiritual and natural gifts were encouraged and empowered to expand the Kingdom of heaven. There were no exceptions, for the harvest was plentiful and the laborers were few.

Upon His resurrection, Jesus returned authority and power to humanity. He did so in order for humans to subdue and rule the earth as God had originally mandated at creation. God didn't take away that mandate since the gifts and callings of God are irrevocable (Romans 11:29). He came to take from the enemy that which we had given away.

The apostle Paul makes a distinction about the role that Adam and Eve played in the Fall. He said that "man sinned" (Romans 5) and gave away his authority to the devil while the woman was deceived (1 Timothy 2) into giving away her authority. It seems to me that intentional sin is a greater wrong than being deceived.

The Bible makes clear that women were re-established as the rightful heirs of God's Kingdom as much as men. Because of the early church's firm belief in the re-establishing of God's original mandate, men and women co-labored as mothers and fathers in the Kingdom to win souls and establish the reality of "on earth as it is in heaven." Jesus came as the Son of Man to conquer evil, take our place at the cross, and return the right to rule to the sons of Adam and daughters of Eve.

The residence of the Holy Spirit living in the bodies of people—who believed in Jesus as the Messiah—is an equalizer. The apostle Paul taught that every distinction peoples and cultures have created to place hierarchical value on individuals and groups were obliterated in Jesus Christ. Jesus bore the sins of the world in His own body and created a new race of people who heaven would recognize as a "new creation."

This new breed of humanity would not only be created in the image of God, but they would also become the living temples of the Spirit of God. There is no lesser Holy Spirit in any born-again Believer. Paul strongly admonished the early church to treat one another as equals and to recognize the God-image-bearing and God-housing nature of all people.

"There is neither Jew nor Greek, there is neither slave nor free, there is no male and female, for you are all one in Christ Jesus." (Galatians 3:28)

Yet, over the course of centuries, especially as Christianity received political favor in the days of Constantine, the world's value system would corrupt the purity of the Kingdom message. One of the first pillars to fall was the belief that men and women both bear the image of God and were both created to rule and reign. Suddenly, the world's norm of subjugating the physically weaker sex would color the lens through which even Christian leaders would read the Bible.

Verses that were meant to address specific issues in specific churches were highlighted and emphasized to oppress women. Stories of women who were leading in the same capacity as the men somehow became the exception. These stories of women in leadership would be swept under the rug of complementarian theology and largely ignored. The theology of complementarianism would be applied all the way back to the creation story.

Rather than seeing that the woman was called a "help-mate," even as God also referred to Himself as man's "help-mate," theologians began to interpret the creation story as if God created the woman as an afterthought. If not an afterthought, theologians would teach that women's function was to make men's lives easier. Women were created to fulfill the desires and destinies of men.

The traditional rabbinic understanding of gender differences and the cultural standards of the day colored Christian theology and practice to the point that there came a time when women were no longer accepted as leaders. They were told to be quiet, to not preach, to submit to their husbands. Thus, the freedom Jesus came to give all humanity was now reserved for men. Women would slowly lose the right to preach, to make administrative decisions, to plant churches, to lead movements and to speak out against injustices.

Now, a millennia and several centuries after the Roman Empire established Christianity as their official religion, the theology of women in leadership is being radically revisited. Should women be allowed to preach? Can women instruct men? The underlying question to these issues is: "Are women truly equal to men?" Did God create women as an afterthought to take away man's loneliness or were women always a part of God's original design? If females are created in the image of God, then females are not inferior. And the feminine nature is also derived from a nature found in the God-head. Women bear the image of the Divine as much as men. Part of the great reformation the Church will go through is to redeem the feminine nature of God and therefore the feminine part of humanity.

In the world, women have already taken positions of supreme power and authority in government, business and education. Women are already shaping the world, making decisions about laws, affecting cultural mores and ruling nations. If we truly believe that, God appoints world rulers (Romans 13), then it stands to reason that it was God who appointed women to also rule and reign.

In order for us to be a relevant voice in this generation, I believe it's imperative for the church to establish mothers in the Kingdom. God repeatedly instructed families to honor their mothers and fathers. It's time for the church to follow God's instructions. Christians cannot continue to marginalize women as inferior creatures. The harvest is too large to effectively handicap half the Body of Christ. We can no longer waste precious time and energy debating whether women can preach on Sundays. Revival and reformation are already upon us. We cannot lose the next generation because of archaic, distorted and misapplied theology.

If we truly believe God's Kingdom is about family, then the church needs to find a way to allow mothers' voices to be as equally crucial as the fathers' voices. The feminine perspective helps balance out the compartmentalized view of life and helps establish the emotional health of the family. When both mothers and fathers speak into their children's lives, the family is at its' optimal health. It is this way because this is God's own design. He wants it this way.

This book is not intended to be a comprehensive study. I'm simply offering a glimpse into why I believe some of the women in the Bible are mentioned and their stories told. The Bible tends to highlight men's stories and their journey with God. For many stories with the same theme for men, there tends to be only a single story of the same theme featuring a woman. There is a hiddenness to the role of women in the Bible, and one has to take the time to discover them. But the fact that they are included shows that God has always factored women into His plans, and their roles tend to be crucial.

I hope this book offers valuable insights into how God saw women, and gave a valid perspective of why women are so important to Jesus. I hope it revealed how time and time again, Jesus's interactions with women showed how much He valued and loved them. How He gave them space and place when the culture and religion of His time would forbid such a thing. How He defied man's culture and religion and revealed Kingdom family. And I hope you see that women truly mattered to the Lord.

This journey with Jesus has been the wildest, craziest, most exciting kind of adventure I could have ever dreamt. The best experiences the world has to offer cannot begin to compare to the brilliance of who Jesus is. When He comes into our life, touches us with His hand of grace, calls us by name, and bestows on us the crown of the "Beloved," we begin the journey to completeness, wholeness, and healing. No love on earth, no matter how giving and unselfish, can come close to the unlimited, unending, unconditional love of Jesus Christ. It's true freedom to know His love.

As a fellow sojourner of faith, I pray blessings over you for favor, grace, and wisdom of Jesus. I pray blessings of love, acceptance, and intimacy with God the Father, God the Son, and God the Holy Spirit. I pray blessings of freedom, purpose and destiny. I pray blessings of divine fulfillment of godly dreams and hopes. I pray that you, your children, and their children and the generations to come will empower girls and women as Jesus did.

"The Lord bless you and keep you, the Lord make His face shine upon you and be gracious to you; the Lord turn His face toward you and give you peace." (Numbers 6:24-25)

Where do we go from here?

Nothing I've written in this book is meant as a complete study. In fact, there are many more strong women and important topics in the Bible that I did not include in this book. For instance, I plan to dig deeper into the lives of other amazing women like the Bethany sisters in future books. Also, nothing I offer is intended to be as a final statement in anything, and that is the point. I offered a glimpse into why I believe some of the women in the Bible are mentioned and their stories told but doing your own deep and personal study on these topics can be so powerful and freeing.

As a woman called into ministry, a mother to three sons, a daughter, and a grandmother to a most beautiful granddaughter, I have the distinct privilege of hearing many people's thoughts and opinions. Also, in this modern age of social media where everyone with internet access can state their opinions without deep research, it's hard to differentiate what is sound theology and what are people's opinions. With all this misinformation flying around, I can see how vast numbers of Christians can mistakenly promote misogyny in the name of Jesus, but it needs to stop.

God, in His great wisdom, brilliance, and grace enables each of us to access some of the world's best teachers of His Word right in our own homes through the magic of the internet and podcasts. I encourage you to take advantage of such awesome opportunities and keep seeking, pursuing, and learning Truth. I tend to repeat this until those around me are probably sick of hearing it, but I must say this again. Truth is a Person. We seek Jesus when we seek Truth and when we seek Him, He is always found. And you may find that He was the one seeking and pursuing you all along.

With that said, I would like to leave you with a few resources that I found helpful as well as a few hot button societal questions for you to do your own research on to dig deeper.

Resources:

Why Not Women ~ David Joel Hamilton and Loren Cunningham

Fashioned to Reign ~ Kris Vallotton

Holding Up Half the Sky: A Biblical Case for Woman Leading the Teaching in the Church ~ Graham Joseph Hill

Powerful And Free: Confronting the Glass Ceiling Women in the Church ~ Danny Silk

Mary and Early Christian Women: Hidden Leadership ~ Ally Kateusz

Questions for deeper study:

- Why does society put so much shame on the women being driven out of the garden and not the man?
- Why do some believe that Paul meant it to be permanent when

he told women to stay quiet in church when in that same chapter he tells them they can prophecy and pray in church?

- Why do some believe that when scripture says man being the head of women means he is to lord over her when in the same verse says God is the head of Jesus and they are equal.

- Why do we take the societal oppression in between as God's design when women are equal to men in the garden and in the afterlife?

ACKNOWLEDGMENTS

To the Wednesday Prayer Group: You have shown me that prayers do move mountains and that fellowship in the Kingdom can be full of joy, adventure, passion and miracles. You're each a favored woman in Jesus' life. You're my family and I love you all so much.

Made in the USA
Coppell, TX
23 October 2020

40188446R00096